Advertising, Competition, and Public Policy

Theories and New Evidence

Robert E. McAuliffe
Babson College

Lexington Books
D.C. Heath and Company/Lexington, Massachusetts/Toronto

Library of Congress Cataloging-in-Publication Data

McAuliffe, Robert E.
  Advertising, competition, and public policy.

  Bibliography: p.
  1. Advertising—United States. 2. Competition—
United States. 3. Advertising—Government policy—
United States. I. Title.
HF5813.U6M33   1987   659.1'0973   85–45896
ISBN 0–669–12391–9 (alk. paper)

Published simultaneously in Canada
Printed in the United States of America
International Standard Book Number: 0–669–12391–9
Library of Congress Catalog Card Number: 85–45896

The paper used in this publication meets the minimum requirements of
American National Standard for Information Sciences—Permanence of
Paper for Printed Library Materials, ANSI Z39.48–1984. ∞™

87 88 89 90 8 7 6 5 4 3 2 1

To Lois

Contents

Figures and Tables

Figures

Tables

Acknowledgments

I owe thanks to many people who have provided direct and indirect support with this project. I am especially grateful to Roger Sherman who carefully reviewed a (very) rough draft of this manuscript in the early stages of the research. His comments improved the clarity and unity of the text throughout. Ken Koford also provided valuable comments on the entire manuscript, forcing me to tighten the arguments and incorporate newer research. The manuscript is much improved thanks to their efforts.

I also benefited from discussions with Jim Meehan and Lawrence Moss. They offered helpful advice and criticism on several occasions. Thanks are also due to Frances Nilsson for her assistance in tracking down several data sources and to Connie Stumpf for xeroxing.

The Babson Board of Research provided invaluable financial support. Completion of this work would have been far more difficult without this assistance.

My greatest debt is to my wife, who made every possible effort to help me complete this study.

1
Introduction

Advertising has always been surrounded by controversy. Public policy in the United States ranges from general oversight (such as Federal Trade Commission investigations of the truthfulness of advertising claims) to bans against advertising specific products (such as the bans against broadcast advertising of cigarettes and liquor). Recently public interest groups and the American Medical Association have called for a complete ban on all cigarette advertising, and proposals have been made to eliminate all broadcast advertising of beer and wine.

A major concern among economists is the effect of advertising expenditures on competition. Initial studies by Kaldor (1950) and Bain (1956) indicated that advertising by large firms reduced competition and made it more difficult for new firms to enter the market. According to this view, advertising insulated established firms from competition and enabled them to earn high profits. But other economists have argued that advertising increases competition by informing consumers about new products. It would be far more difficult for new firms to enter a new market if they could not advertise to let consumers know about their product.

Although several reviews of this research have appeared in the literature, many recent developments in the areas of strategic deterrence, consistent conjectures, barriers to entry, and the information theories of advertising have not been systematically reviewed. One purpose of this study is to provide a survey of the theoretical issues in the advertising debate incorporating these new developments. A crucial issue is whether advertising reduces competition in markets or increases it. From the survey of the literature presented in chapters 2 and 3, several important issues about the competitive effects of advertising are clarified, and testable hypotheses are derived.

Causation versus Correlation

The causal relation between advertising and measures of market power has been a controversial point in the advertising debate. Many researchers have discovered a positive correlation between advertising levels and accounting profits, yet this correlation does not prove that advertising is the cause of higher profits. Several theoretical models have been developed which show that the correlation between advertising and profits may be due to other factors, and these models are discussed in chapter 3.[1]

To illustrate the problem, consider a profit-maximizing monopolist who advertises in the market. From the first-order conditions for a profit maximum we know that:

$$(P - MC)/P = -1/\eta, \tag{1.1}$$

where P is the price of the product, MC is the marginal cost of production, and η is the elasticity of demand for the product. Many researchers have interpreted the positive correlation between advertising and profits as evidence that advertising reduces competition, reduces the firm's elasticity of demand in equation 1.1, and causes profits to increase. However, the same profit-maximizing monopolist will also advertise until the following condition holds:

$$A/S = -\eta_a/\eta, \tag{1.2}$$

where A/S is the ratio of advertising expenditures to sales, and η_a is the advertising elasticity of demand (see chapter 3). This is the Dorfman–Steiner condition for the optimal level of advertising by a monopolist.[2] Since the market elasticity of demand appears in equations 1.1 and 1.2, it is possible that the correlation between advertising and profits occurs because both variables respond to changes in the elasticity of demand. If this interpretation is correct, there may be no causal connection between advertising and profits despite positive correlations between these variables. Certainly the possibility of spurious correlation between advertising and profits weakens the causal interpretation of the evidence.

In this study the causal relationship between advertising and market power is tested directly. Granger (1969) developed an operational definition of causality based upon timing relations in the data. Several features of the causal tests are ideally suited for testing the causal effects of advertising, and in chapter 5 these tests are described and implemented to determine how advertising affects market power. The results of these tests also provide information about appropriate estimation techniques in advertising studies. Many studies have simply regressed profits against advertising levels and other variables, yet this procedure yields biased estimates if advertising is not exogenous.

Measurement Issues

Many advertising studies have used accounting profit data as a proxy for economic profits. Since competitive firms cannot persistently earn high economic profits, high accounting profits have been considered a signal of monopoly power. However, this approach is valid only if accounting profits accurately measure economic profits, and Fisher and McGowan (1983) showed that accounting profit data provide almost no information about economic profits. Although their conclusions were criticized, Fisher (1984) demonstrated that accounting profit data can bias statistical tests even in cases where this data is a good proxy for economic profits. To test for the competitive effects of advertising, an observable measure of market power is needed. Thus in chapter 4 we present an alternative approach to measuring market power that is suitable for the tests.

Another measurement problem concerns advertising expenditures. Most of the previous research in advertising has used industrywide data on profits and advertising–sales ratios to determine the effects of advertising on competition. However, this level of aggregation can bias the tests, as we will argue in chapter 4. A new source of advertising expenditures by firm is employed in this study to avoid this problem. Furthermore, a price index of advertising costs is developed for each firm in the sample. No other research has analyzed the effects of real advertising expenditures at this level of detail, and these improved measures should increase the accuracy of the tests.

The Effects of Advertising Restrictions

Federal law banned broadcast advertising of cigarettes in 1971, and numerous studies have investigated the effectiveness of advertising bans in reducing consumption. In chapter 6 several theoretical models are presented to determine the effects of an advertising ban on welfare. A surprising result is that these bans are likely to reduce social welfare unless there are sizable externalities in the market.

Despite the large volume of research on the effects of advertising restrictions on cigarette demand, many of the estimates are biased. The demand for cigarettes has often been estimated by ordinary least squares, but this procedure is biased when prices and quantities are endogenous. Many studies of cigarette demand failed to identify the demand curve as well, so it is not clear that the effects of the advertising ban have been correctly assessed. Several studies are reviewed in chapter 6 to develop a theoretical specification for cigarette demand, and new estimates of the effectiveness of advertising restrictions are presented.

Notes

1. See Sherman and Tollison (1971), Nelson (1974), and Ehrlich and Fisher (1982).

2. See Dorfman and Steiner (1954) and chapter 3.

2
Advertising as a Barrier to Entry

According to economic theory, unusually high profits cannot persist in a competitive industry because high returns will attract new firms and this will increase output. Ultimately the increase in output will reduce the price of the product and industry returns will fall to normal (competitive, risk-adjusted) levels. Even a monopolist cannot earn high returns for long if new firms can freely enter the market and compete for those profits. Competition from new firms will eventually eliminate monopoly profits.

The conclusion that excess profits will be eliminated by competition depends upon the relative ease of entry into different industries. If it is difficult to enter an industry, established firms may be able to earn returns above those that could be earned elsewhere. According to some economists, if firms are persistently able to earn high returns above the competitive level, there must be barriers to entry in that industry.

In this chapter we will analyze the role of advertising as an entry barrier. The crucial issue is whether advertising by established firms can raise profits and prevent new firms from entering the industry. Several theories have been developed which assert that advertising can reduce competition in markets and they are discussed and critically examined in this chapter. Many disagreements over the effects of advertising on competition are due to differences in the definition of entry barriers. Therefore in the section "What Are Barriers to Entry?" barriers to entry are defined and several avenues by which advertising may increase entry barriers are presented. Since economies of scale are considered by some economists to be a barrier to entry, we examine the role of advertising in creating economies of scale in the section "Economies of Scale in Advertising." Asymmetries that can be created by advertising in favor of established firms are treated in "Asymmetries in Demand Caused by Advertising," and in "Strategic Entry Deterrence with Advertising," issues regarding strategic entry deterrence are analyzed. The concept of entry barriers is reconsidered in "Other Issues Concerning Barriers to Entry," and an appraisal of the research on advertising as a barrier to entry appears in the "Conclusions" section. Advertising may create entry barriers in specific cases, but current research does not support the position that advertising always (or often) reduces competition. Therefore public policy toward advertising must proceed on a case-by-case basis.

What Are Barriers to Entry?

The concept of entry barriers was originally developed by Bain (1956). He argued that a barrier to entry exists when established firms have advantages over potential entrants. These advantages allow established firms to earn profits that exceed the competitive rate of return without attracting entry. High profits are not only a signal of entry barriers, they also measure the height of the entry barriers. Since high rates of return are more likely to attract entry, the higher the profit rate of established firms, the higher the entry barrier. Comanor and Wilson (1974) have argued:

> Where entry barriers are important and persist over time, established firms can reach an *equilibrium* position in which excess profits are earned. These higher returns represent an economic rent, but one associated with the market power of a firm rather than with a scarce input in the production process.[1]

Bain and others have argued that advertising is a source of entry barriers. According to Comanor and Wilson, advertising can raise entry barriers in any or all of the following ways:

1. There could be economies of scale in advertising effectiveness.
2. Advertising could create absolute cost advantages for established firms because entrants must advertise more than established firms.
3. Advertising might create economies of scale in costs (if the unit costs of advertising decline as expenditures on advertising increase).
4. Advertising might create product differentiation advantages for established firms.

The concept of economies of scale refers to the relationship between the costs of producing output and the scale of the operation (the amount of capital, labor, and raw material inputs used in production). If all inputs in the production process (including the size of the plant) are doubled and output more than doubles, there are economies of scale in production. It is important to note that economies of scale refers to the changes in output that occur when *all* inputs are changed in the same proportion. It is also possible for output to more than double when a *single* input in the production process is doubled. In this case there are increasing returns to that input. Increasing returns and economies of scale are not the same, although several economists in the advertising debate have ignored the distinction.[2]

When there are economies of scale in production, firms must achieve a large sales volume to reduce costs. According to Bain, this makes entry into an industry more difficult since new firms are generally smaller than established firms. If the new firms enter at a small scale they will have higher costs, and if they enter at a large scale, the additional output will cause the market price to fall drastically, reducing profits for all firms. In either case, new entrants will be discouraged by economies of scale.

Product differentiation is another means by which advertising can create entry barriers. Bain and his followers assert that advertising causes physically similar products to appear different from each other. This differentiation reduces the elasticity of demand for a product and makes consumers less willing to substitute other brands or products for the advertised brand. As a result, advertising allows firms to raise product prices and earn monopoly profits because it reduces competition.

Advertising may also increase barriers to entry by creating brand loyalty. When brand loyalty exists, an entering firm must overcome the preference consumers have for the established brands. This may require new entrants to advertise more than established firms or to offer other inducements (such as lower prices) to encourage brand switching. Any strategy necessary to overcome brand loyalty will reduce the entrant's expected profits and this may deter entry.

If advertising does create barriers to entry, then high levels of advertising should lead to higher profits. Many econometric studies have examined the relationship between advertising and profits across industries.[3] Generally these studies have found a positive relationship between these two variables, apparently confirming the hypothesis that advertising creates barriers to entry. However, there is still considerable doubt among economists concerning the interpretation of these findings. This issue will be discussed in more detail in chapters 3 and 4. For our present purposes it is sufficient to acknowledge that a positive relationship between advertising and profits has been confirmed by some empirical work, and that Bain's followers view this evidence as support for the hypothesis that advertising reduces competition.

Although Bain's definition of barriers to entry has been used by many researchers, his is not the only definition that appears in the literature. Stigler (1983) has defined an entry barrier as a "cost of producing (at some or every rate of output) which must be borne by a firm which seeks to enter an industry but is not borne by firms already in the industry."[4] Stigler argues that economies of scale are *not* a barrier to entry because potential entrants have access to the same cost conditions. If a new firm cannot enter an industry because the market is not large enough to accommodate both the new firm and established firms, the problem is the size of the market, not entry barriers. Certainly it is not the fault of the established firms that costs decline over a large range of output levels. Yet many economists who assert that economies of scale are a barrier to entry recommend policies that would restrict the actions of established firms with declining costs.

The definition of an entry barrier is crucial because the models and tests economists develop to determine the effects of advertising will depend upon the definition of entry barriers employed. If advertising is less costly or becomes more effective as the size of the advertising budget is increased, then those who use Bain's definition of entry barriers will assert that advertising is anticompetitive because it makes entry into the industry more difficult. These economists would then develop tests to determine the social costs of advertising. However, according to the definition used by Stigler, there is no barrier to entry even if advertising costs decline because the costs decline for all firms, including potential entrants. Therefore entrants are not at a disadvantage relative to established firms, and economists using Stigler's definition would not test for anticompetitive effects in this case.

The definition of entry barriers is also important for antitrust analysis. Since Bain's definition of entry barriers is much broader than Stigler's, many more business practices will be condemned as anticompetitive using Bain's approach. If these practices clearly reduce competition, then antitrust actions may be justified. However, if these practices simply appear to create entry barriers, and the courts are persuaded by the evidence, the courts may incorrectly penalize innocent firms. Economists will use different tests and theories to settle antitrust cases and they will interpret the evidence obtained according to the definition of entry barriers they employ. Although Stigler's definition seems to be gaining acceptance, the issue is still in dispute.[5] With this in mind, we will discuss the role of advertising as an entry barrier in more detail.

Economies of Scale in Advertising

Although economies of scale are not considered to be entry barriers by Stigler, they play an important role for Bain's followers. Therefore in this section we will consider the issue of economies of scale in advertising in more detail. A simple production function is presented to illustrate the important issues in the debate concerning the role of economies of scale in advertising.

A production function is often used to describe the relationship between the inputs used in production and the quantity of output produced. A common production function in economics is the Cobb-Douglas production function. It describes the output produced in physical units, q, as a function of the capital, K, and labor, L, inputs,

$$q = AK^\alpha L^\beta, \tag{2.1}$$

where A is a variable representing the effects of technology. Economies of scale exist when $\alpha + \beta > 1$. In this case, if we double the inputs in production, output will rise by $2^{\alpha+\beta}$.[6]

Despite the importance of economies of scale in the advertising debate, it has been difficult to measure and test for them. The problem arises because the concept of economies of scale refers to the change in output that occurs when *all* factors of production are increased. If we found that output more than doubled when all inputs in production were doubled, how could we determine if advertising *alone* caused the additional increase in output? As Simon and Arndt (1983) have argued, it makes little sense to attempt to isolate the effects of advertising expenditures (or any other single input) on scale economies, since the concept refers to the effects of changing all inputs simultaneously.

Empirical studies that have estimated economies of scale due to advertising have also been hampered by data problems. Generally data are gathered from firms that vary in size (but not scale). The problem is that larger firms generally do not use inputs in the same proportion as smaller firms. Therefore other variables can be responsible for changes in output in addition to variations in the scale of the operation. For example, Simon and Arndt (1983) suggest that larger firms might have more extensive distribution channels than smaller firms. If so, this difference between large and small firms could explain why larger firms have higher sales with fewer inputs, not economies of scale. With these problems of measurement and data collection, Simon and Arndt conclude that it is impossible to determine in practice whether advertising is responsible for economies of scale.

Since we cannot measure economies of scale due to advertising alone, is it possible that advertising confers advantages to larger firms in some other fashion? Larger firms might enjoy advantages over smaller firms if there are increasing returns to advertising, because increases in advertising could generate even larger increases in sales, holding other inputs constant. There are two sources of increasing returns to advertising: The effectiveness of advertising increases as the number of advertising messages increases (these are "real" sources of increasing returns) or the unit cost of an advertising message declines because of price discounts to large advertisers (which are "pecuniary" sources of increasing returns).

As Simon and Arndt (1980, 1983) have noted, the first source of increasing returns refers to the response of sales to advertising expenditures. If the percentage increase in sales is greater than the percentage increase in advertising, there are increasing returns to advertising. In this situation, entrants must advertise heavily to overcome the more effective advertising expenditures of established firms, and this places new firms at a disadvantage. After an extensive review of the research on the response of sales to advertising, however, Simon and Arndt (1980) concluded that there are *diminishing returns* to advertising. The bulk of the evidence indicates that increases in advertising generate less than proportionate increases in sales. Even Comanor and Wilson (1980) accept this finding. Therefore it appears that entry barriers are not caused by increasing real returns to advertising (using Bain's concept of entry barriers).

Another way advertising could generate increasing returns is if the costs of advertising fall as the advertising budget increases due to pecuniary economies of scale. However, given that there are diminishing returns to advertising, it is not clear that increasing returns can be generated by media discounts. Larger advertisers generally spend less per unit of advertising, but these discounts may not be sufficient to offset the reduced effectiveness of additional advertising messages due to diminishing returns. If larger advertisers have lower unit costs per message but the messages are less effective, we cannot be certain that they have an advantage over smaller firms. The evidence on the effects of media discounts as a source of scale economies is mixed,[7] suggesting that even if discounts create advantages for large firms, the effects are not substantial. As a result we must conclude that the evidence does not support the view that advertising creates advantages for large firms via increasing returns.

Further support for the view that advertising does not create significant cost advantages for large firms was recently provided in a study by Schmalensee, Silk, and Bojanek (1983). They examined the costs of advertising for advertising agencies to determine whether economies of scale exist. Since the agencies in their sample varied in size rather than scale, the study more accurately measures the significance of economies of size in advertising. They found that economies of size are exhausted at small output levels relative to the size of most advertising agencies. Therefore they conclude that economies of size for advertising agencies do not generate economically significant decreases in advertising costs after agencies have reached a comparatively small size.

A different approach to the issue of advertising and economies of scale has recently been developed by Spence (1980). He argues that advertising can create a barrier to entry because it can lead to economies of scale in generating revenues. Previous research has focused on the issue of whether the firm's costs of advertising decline with increases in the amount of advertising. The results have been mixed, with some economists asserting that there are decreasing costs in advertising (see Brown [1978]) while others have found no such effects (see Simon [1980]). The point Spence raises is that it is not sufficient to determine whether the per unit costs of advertising decline with increases in output. Rather, it is necessary to consider the interaction of advertising with the other inputs of production and distribution together to determine if scale economies exist.

To see Spence's point, consider the Cobb–Douglas production function presented earlier. Scale economies exist in producing output if $\alpha + \beta > 1$ below,

$$q = AK^\alpha L^\beta, \qquad (2.2)$$

where q is output. Spence asserts that scale economies may exist in generating revenues, not output, when advertising is required for sales. The i-th firm faces the following inverse demand function in the market:

$$p_i = B(m)A(a_i)q_i^{\alpha - 1}, \qquad (2.3)$$

where q_i is the i-th firm's output, $B(m)$ is a scale factor that varies across firms, and $A(a_i)$ represents the effect of advertising by the i-th firm (a_i) on demand. Profits are

$$\pi_i = B(m)A(a_i)q_i^\alpha - [c(q_i) + a_i], \qquad (2.4)$$

where $c(q_i)$ is the cost function for the firm. The first term on the right-hand side above represents the revenues of the i-th firm (p_iq_i) and the second term reflects the firm's production and advertising costs. To see how scale economies can arise in generating revenues, let $A = ba^{1/\gamma}$, and $z = q^\beta$. Then profits can be written as:

$$\pi_i = B(m)ba_i^{1/\gamma}z_i^{\alpha/\beta} - (cz_i + a_i), \qquad (2.5)$$

where revenues are $B(m)ba_i^{1/\gamma}z^{\alpha/\beta}$. This revenue function is similar to the Cobb-Douglas production function. Here the advertising (a_i) and output produced (z_i) are the inputs used to generate the output which is revenue. Advertising is an input necessary to obtain sales revenues, and there are economies of scale in generating revenues if $1/\gamma + \alpha/\beta > 1$ which does *not* require increasing returns to either production or advertising alone. Spence argues that larger firms may have advantages over smaller entrants when advertising is necessary to generate revenues and there are economies of scale in generating revenue.

Furthermore, Spence asserts that larger firms can exploit this advantage by creating entry barriers. Established firms can select the optimal level of revenues (by adjusting their advertising and output) so that any firm that tries to enter the industry will be unable to obtain sufficient revenues at a low enough cost to compete. If this strategy successfully prevents new firms from entering the industry, then advertising is a barrier to entry that reduces competition and raises profits for the established firms.

Although the model developed by Spence is intriguing, there are several factors omitted that make entry deterrence much more difficult than the model implies. As Dixit (1982) and Schmalensee (1983) have indicated, advertising will deter entry only if entrants believe that established firms will maintain their advertising at the same level when entry occurs. However, in some cases profit maximization requires the established firms to advertise *less* when entry is possible, and this makes it more difficult for them to deter entry with advertising. (See the discussion on strategic entry deterrence in "Strategic Entry Deterrence with Advertising.")

Another issue concerns the nature of the demand function in the model. Demand is fixed in Spence's model, which makes entry more difficult and entry deterrence more likely. When markets are expanding and demand is increasing, it is much more difficult for established firms to prevent entry. In a growing market entrants can achieve the sales volume required by economies of scale, when they exist, without necessarily reducing the sales of established firms. In this case retaliation by established firms is less likely and so they are less able to deter entry.

Furthermore, there is no uncertainty in Spence's model. Established firms know the demand curve in the market and use that knowledge (combined with possible economies of scale) to deter entry. When market conditions are uncertain, the payoffs from a strategy of entry deterrence are less obvious. Established firms may not even be able to find the optimal entry deterring strategy if conditions in the market are constantly changing or uncertain.

Finally, as Schmalensee (1974) and Needham (1976) have argued, the fact that established firms may be able to deter entry does not necessarily mean that it is profitable for them to do so. Established firms may find that their long-run profits are higher if they allow entry to occur when the costs of entry deterrence are high. It is not sufficient to show that advertising (or other strategies) *could* deter entry; it must be shown that these strategies are *likely* to be profitable for those firms that pursue them.

Asymmetries in Demand Caused by Advertising

Entry deterrence requires some asymmetries between established firms and entrants. If firms entering an industry face exactly the same demand and cost conditions as established firms, how can established firms ever prevent entry? Without differences in demand or cost conditions between established firms and entrants, entry deterrence is impossible.[8] In the preceding section we concluded that there are diminishing returns to advertising and that it is impossible to determine whether advertising *alone* is responsible for economies of scale. Therefore it is difficult to establish that advertising creates cost advantages for established firms. However, advertising may create advantages for established firms if it creates asymmetries in demand. This might occur if consumers are more responsive to advertising by established firms. In this section we will examine several models where advertising might create advantages for established brands.

One argument presented by Bain (1956), Comanor and Wilson (1974), and others is that advertising provides established firms with advantages over potential entrants because it creates brand loyalty. Any new firm that tries to enter the market must overcome the preference consumers have for the established brands. As in the case with increasing returns, brand loyalty requires entrants to advertise more heavily than established firms, and this places entrants at a competitive disadvantage. Brand loyalty created by advertising allows established firms to raise their prices and increase profits without attracting entry. Therefore advertising raises entry barriers when it creates brand loyalty according to Bain's definition of barriers to entry.

Schmalensee (1974) tried to provide a more rigorous treatment of the effects of brand loyalty created by advertising to support this view. Surprisingly, he found that when advertising creates brand loyalty, it does *not* raise entry barriers under plausible conditions. Although the model is complicated, the reasoning is straightforward. If advertising in previous years caused consumers to be loyal to the brand today, the value of the firm would be increased by the "goodwill" created by past advertising. The firm can reap the rewards from this goodwill by earning higher profits in the future from loyal customers or by selling the firm today at a higher price that reflects the present value of this goodwill.

The important point in this model is that the value of this goodwill is like a fixed-income bond. The returns received from this investment have no effect on the profitability of any activity the firm undertakes today. That is, decisions made by the firm today should not be affected by the value of past advertising. The firm will receive the same income from advertising goodwill whether it raises or lowers its current advertising budget. In this respect the benefits from goodwill are similar to fixed costs: their existence has no effect on short-run marginal decisions.

Since the value of past advertising does not affect the current decisions made by established firms, it cannot affect their response when entry occurs.[9] If the goodwill earned by the established firms does not affect their reaction to new firms, then brand loyalty created by advertising is not a barrier to entry. Barriers to entry must be caused by other differences between established firms and entrants (such as product quality); they are not caused by brand loyalty from advertising.

Comanor and Wilson (1979) challenged this conclusion. While they agreed that advertising cannot restrict entry simply because it has durable effects, they also argued that advertising was more effective for established firms because consumers were more familiar with their products. Furthermore, they argued that Schmalensee's comparison of the goodwill from past advertising with a fixed-income bond was incorrect. The returns from a fixed-income bond do not affect current decisions made by the firm, but goodwill from past advertising *does* affect current decisions. After all, the only way the firm can enjoy the "income" from advertising goodwill is to raise current prices to earn higher profits. Since Schmalensee initially assumed that price–cost margins were constant and the same for all firms in his model, established firms could never reap the rewards from their goodwill. Therefore Comanor and Wilson conclude that his model fails to capture the effects of advertising as an entry barrier.

While these criticisms raised by Comanor and Wilson are correct, they do not affect Schmalensee's conclusions. For example, Schmalensee relaxes the assumption of identical price–cost margins (1974, p. 583) and allows the established firms to earn higher markups than those earned by entrants. However, even if advertising enables established firms to set higher prices for their products, they are no more able to deter entry than before. In fact, the higher markups will make entry more likely since the potential rewards to new firms are higher.

The other criticism raised by Comanor and Wilson is also correct: advertising goodwill is not like a bond because it does affect current pricing decisions. However, this criticism does not affect the validity of Schmalensee's results. It is true that the firm must raise prices and earn higher profits to reap the benefits from past advertising. But this does not increase the power established firms have to *prevent* entry, and this is the crucial issue raised by Schmalensee. Brand loyalty created by advertising does not give established firms any additional power to prevent entry and therefore it does not change the entry conditions faced by new firms.[10]

The issue raised here is important and deserves further consideration because it reflects crucial differences in the approach to entry barriers. According to Bain, a barrier to entry exists when established firms earn economic profits without attracting entry. Therefore, Comanor and Wilson assert, if advertising creates brand loyalty and allows established firms to raise their prices above marginal cost, a barrier to entry exists. For Schmalensee, the issue is whether brand loyalty created by advertising allows established firms to actively prevent entry. In his model, brand loyalty deters entry only if it increases the power established firms have to drive an entrant's profits to zero while they earn positive profits. When incumbent firms earn positive profits but cannot deter entry, there is no barrier caused by brand loyalty according to Schmalensee's logic. If incumbent firms are no more able to prevent entry by advertising, then advertising does not create entry barriers.

This disagreement illustrates the importance of the definition of entry barriers, and how economists can reach very different conclusions from the same model when using alternative definitions. Although Bain's definition is widely used by economists, it may be misleading to assume the presence of entry barriers simply because an industry earns high profits. High accounting profits in any industry do not necessarily imply that established firms are deliberately preventing entry. Nor do such profits indicate that there is some failure in the market that must be corrected to improve entry conditions. For example, a firm might have an excellent location that lowers its transportation costs. These lower transportation costs might enable the firm to earn higher measured profits, but these may not be economic profits if the true value of the location is not included in the asset value of the firm. What appears to be economic profit in this case is actually a rent that has not been capitalized. In Schmalensee's model advertising goodwill is an asset whose value is not properly accounted for on the firm's balance sheet. If the true value of the goodwill were added to the asset base of the firm, measured profits would fall.[11] In cases such as this, accounting profits may not accurately measure economic profits.

High accounting profits indicate the presence of entry barriers only to the extent that they measure economic profits.[12] If other factors are responsible for high accounting profits, it is incorrect to conclude that barriers to entry are present. For example, Comanor and Wilson (1974) argue that potential entrants do not face the same demand conditions as established firms because consumers are less familiar with new products. As a result of this uncertainty, advertising by established firms is more effective than advertising by new entrants and this is a barrier to entry. However, they overlook an important issue: What is the real barrier to entry? If consumers are uncertain about product quality and are therefore more responsive to advertisements for established brands, is advertising the problem? While Comanor and Wilson seem to imply that advertising is the villain, the real source of the difficulty is uncertainty. When advertising by established firms is more effective than entrants' advertising because consumers are not familiar with the new products, this is the cost of uncertainty. If uncertainty increases the effectiveness of advertising by established firms, this has nothing to do with advertising *creating* a barrier to entry or reducing competition.[13] Yet Comanor and Wilson interpret a positive correlation between accounting profits and advertising as evidence that advertising must reduce competition.

Certainly if established firms only advertised to prevent entry, the resources used in that effort would be wasted from society's viewpoint. If advertising goodwill enabled established firms to prevent entry, and if advertising resources were used only for deterrence, then some policy action limiting advertising might be justified on efficiency grounds if the costs of intervention do not exceed the benefits. However, it is not clear that policy actions are justified whenever high profits are observed, and in this respect the broad view of entry barriers can be misleading. High entry barriers should enable firms to earn higher returns, but the existence of high returns does not necessarily imply the existence of entry barriers.

Can advertising create *any* asymmetries between established firms and entrants? From the analysis presented thus far in this chapter it might appear that the answer is no, but this is not true. Despite the criticisms presented against the view that advertising creates a barrier to entry in general, it is possible that advertising prevents entry in specific cases. However, the criticisms raised require advocates of the barrier-to-entry hypothesis to focus their attention on specific instances where advertising is known to reduce competition. When advertising expenditures do reduce competition, they should also raise the future stream of profits earned by the firm, and this hypothesis can be tested, as we will show in chapter 5. At this point broad policies that restrict advertising across entire industries have not yet received strong theoretical and empirical support. We shall see in the following section that established firms do have certain strategic advantages over entrants, although these advantages are not created by advertising alone.

Strategic Entry Deterrence with Advertising

Established firms may have a strategic advantage over potential entrants even when both firms face the same postentry demand and cost conditions. The advantage occurs because established firms are in a leadership position that enables them to take actions prior to entry that place the entrant at a strategic disadvantage. Salop (1979) refers to this advantage as a *preentry asymmetry*. Although the established firms and the potential entrant are equally matched after entry occurs, the established firm may be able to improve its position before entry by making binding commitments. In these cases the established firm has "first-move" advantages.

In this section several theories of strategic entry deterrence using advertising will be analyzed. We will consider the possibility that first-move advantages may deter entry by exploring a recent model by Cubbin (1981). In his model, established firms may prevent entry by threatening to increase their advertising after entry occurs. However, if preentry threats are to be believed, potential entrants must expect that established firms will carry out the threats after entry. This constrains the threats established firms can credibly make as well as the models relevant for analyzing entry deterrence. These models are discussed later in the section.

To illustrate the first-move advantages created by advertising, consider the recent model by Cubbin where there is one established firm (this assumption has no effect on the results; there could be several established firms) and one entrant. The established firm is denoted by the subscript 1 and the potential entrant by the subscript 2 for convenience. Established firms are identical to potential entrants in terms of the cost and demand conditions facing each firm. The market demand curve is given by

$$p_i = p(q_i, q_j, A_i, A_j) \qquad i,j = 1,2 \qquad (2.6)$$

where p_i is the price received by the i-th firm, q_i is the quantity sold, and A_i represents advertising expenditure. The demand curve is assumed to have the following properties:

$$\partial p_i / \partial q_i < 0; \quad \partial p_i / \partial q_j < 0; \quad \partial p_i / \partial A_i > 0; \quad \partial p_i / \partial A_j < 0 \qquad (2.7)$$

These conditions simply state that an increase in output by either firm will lower the price received by that firm and by that firm's competitor(s). An increase in advertising will raise the demand for the firm's product but will lower the demand for the competitor's product. Production costs depend upon the firm's output: $c_i = c(q_i)$, and profits for the established firm before entry will be

$$\pi_1 = p(q_1, 0, A_1, 0)q_1 - c(q_1) - A_1. \qquad (2.8)$$

Before entering the market, the entrant must consider the response of the established firm to entry. If the established firm is expected to raise output or increase advertising, the entrant's anticipated profits from entry will be reduced (given the conditions in equation 2.7). Suppose that the entrant's expectations of the established firm's output and advertising response to entry are given by $f(q_1)$ and $g(A_1)$, respectively (where $f > 0$, $f' > 0$, $g > 0$, $g' > 0$). These conditions simply mean that the potential entrant expects the established firm to produce output and advertise after entry occurs. The entrant's expected profits after entry are then

$$\pi_2 = p[q_2, f(q_1), A_2, g(A_1)]q_2 - c(q_2) - A_2. \qquad (2.9)$$

According to Bain's definition, entry is deterred when equation 2.8 is positive (economic profits are earned) but equation 2.9 is negative. The final outcome clearly depends on the nature of the demand, cost, and expectations functions. However, comparing equation 2.8 with equation 2.9, it is clear that the entrant faces a more restricted level of demand than the established firm due to the negative cross effects given in equation 2.7. As long as the entrant expects the established firm to produce output and to advertise after entry, its expected sales are reduced. Therefore Cubbin states that there is a fundamental asymmetry enjoyed by the established firm. Advertising can create a barrier to entry as long as a potential entrant expects the established firm to advertise after entry [$g(A_1) > 0$], an extremely weak condition. Since the established firm is in the market first, it can affect the entrant's profits by changing its output and advertising decisions and this creates first-move advantages for the established firm.

For Cubbin, this asymmetry *alone* is proof that advertising can create barriers to entry, even when there are no differences in the cost functions or demand functions of the established firm and the potential entrant. Since no explicit assumptions about the functional forms of the demand and cost curves were needed to obtain these results, the conclusions appear to be quite robust. Cubbin then argues that the established firms can use this fundamental advantage to exclude entrants via optimal advertising and output strategies. It is important to note, however, that advertising alone is not responsible for this advantage; established firms are favored simply because they appeared in the market first.

One problem with Cubbin's model concerns the specification of the profit function for the established firm in equation 2.8. While it is true that the established firm does not face competition in the *current* period, its output and pricing decisions are affected by potential competition in the future. Since the established firm seeks to prevent entry and the erosion of its profits, it must also anticipate the output and advertising decisions of potential future rivals when considering the optimal profit-maximizing strategy.

For example, suppose that an established firm faces demand and cost conditions such that it is more profitable to allow entry to take place, or that entry should be slowed but not prevented. In deciding on its optimal output and advertising strategy the established firm must weigh the costs of deterring entry (raising output and/or advertising) against the expected benefits of entry deterrence (higher profits). This requires that the established firm consider the possible actions that an entrant might take. But this also limits the "fundamental asymmetry" Cubbin argued must exist because the established firm also faces a restricted level of demand when determining its optimal strategies for output and advertising. If we can characterize the established firm's assumptions about the levels of output and advertising of the potential entrant by the functions $f(q_2)$ and $g(A_2)$ respectively, then the established firm's profits are:

$$\pi_1 = p[q_1, f(q_2), A_1, g(A_2)]q_1 - c(q_1) - A_1 \qquad (2.10)$$

and the asymmetry between established firms and potential entrants is reduced since the profit functions in equations 2.9 and 2.10 are quite similar. All that equation 2.10 states is that the established firm considers potential competition when trying to maximize profits over the long run. Cubbin's analysis overlooks this point because his model is static. He assumes that the established firm maximizes only current profits, yet the process of entry into an industry is dynamic and requires a multiperiod model. Despite this criticism, the established firm still has first-move advantages, but it is more restricted in its ability to use them since it must consider the reactions of potential competitors.

Cubbin's conclusions are less general for yet another reason: demand is assumed to be fixed. A common assumption (implicit or explicit) in most models of entry barriers is that a crucial factor is held constant or fixed. In the models developed by Cubbin (1981) and Spence (1980), market size is constant; in other models variables such as an input in production are held constant. The result is that established firms have advantages because they have already acquired the necessary inputs or market share which, by assumption, leaves less available for potential entrants. Yet market growth can make entry much easier and entry deterrence much more difficult since the entrant can then increase its sales without reducing the sales of the established firms. The negative cross effects from the established firms' advertising and output decisions are much weaker when markets are growing.

Finally, as Schmalensee (1983) has noted, both Spence (1980) and Cubbin (1981) model the effects of advertising as a barrier to entry by analyzing the preentry equilibrium only. They do not consider how established firms would react if entry did occur, and simply argue that advertising by established firms will increase after entry. However, it may not be profitable for established firms to react this way. If the entrant does not believe the established firms' threat to increase advertising after entry takes place, then the threat is not credible and it will not affect the entrant's decision. A threat can only be credible if established firms find it optimal to carry it out in the postentry equilibrium. When Schmalensee modeled the postentry equilibrium with advertising, he obtained a startling result: an established monopolist would *always* advertise less when threatened by entry than when no entry threat existed. In his model, if established firms want to deter entry, they should reduce advertising expenditures, not raise them. Although these results are not completely general, they show that it is more difficult to deter entry with advertising than previous research has indicated, despite the brand loyalty and first-move advantages enjoyed by the established firms.

When firms can invest in capital equipment, there are incentives to overinvest in capital to deter entry.[14] Therefore it is surprising that in Schmalensee's model firms sometimes find it best to underinvest in advertising to deter entry. The difference between the two cases hinges upon the commitment created by the investment. A threat by established firms to increase output and reduce prices will not be taken seriously by potential entrants when this strategy reduces the established firms' profits after entry has occurred. If the decision to increase output can be reversed after entry occurs, established firms have no incentive to carry out their threats unless it is profitable to do so. Knowing this, a potential entrant will not be prevented from entering the industry unless the threats are credible (believable). To make their threats credible, established firms must commit themselves *before* entry in some binding way, as Salop (1979) and Dixit (1982) have emphasized.

When an established firm overinvests in capacity, it commits itself to higher output levels and lower prices in response to entry. Then, if entry occurs, the established firm cannot reduce output and accommodate the entrant because of its irreversible capacity decision. This deters potential entrants because the capacity commitment makes the threat of a price war credible, as Dixit (1980) and Spence (1977) have shown. A preentry commitment made by the incumbent firms can deter entry because it forces the established firms to react aggressively (reduce their prices, increase output) when a new firm enters the market.

Since established firms cannot commit themselves to maintain their advertising levels after entry, these threats are not generally credible. Unlike capacity choice, advertising decisions can be reversed in the current period and are therefore less likely to be carried out if entry occurs. Despite threats to the contrary, an established firm will not increase its advertising after entry if it is not profitable to do so, and it is difficult for established firms to make binding commitments before entry occurs to change this situation. Therefore potential entrants will not believe threats made by established firms to increase advertising after entry occurs unless this action increases their profits. Advertising threats cannot credibly deter entry unless this condition holds.

Why would established firms sometimes find it best to advertise *less* when threatened by entry? In the model developed by Schmalensee (1983), investment in advertising is similar to investment in capital stock in that it is long lived. When the incumbent firm overinvests in advertising capital, it has a larger group of loyal or "captive" customers who will not sample the entrant's product because they are unaware of it. A large captive market reduces the established firm's incentives to respond aggressively to entry. When the established firm reduces price and raises advertising, it sacrifices profits it could earn from its captive market because it must reduce the price for all customers, including those who would only buy from the incumbent. This makes the established firm reluctant to compete and leads to the "fat-cat effect" described by Fudenberg and Tirole (1984). Overinvestment in advertising makes the incumbent fat and lazy when entry occurs, and this makes entry *more* attractive to the entrant who knows that the incumbent will not respond aggressively. In this case, the incumbent firm is better able to deter entry by *underinvesting* in advertising capital relative to the monopoly solution. By underinvesting in advertising capital the incumbent firm establishes a credible threat to reduce prices and increase advertising after entry occurs.

When advertising creates goodwill capital, it has two effects on the behavior of potential entrants in these models. First, advertising will reduce the share of the market available to the entrant by increasing the goodwill of the established firm. This effect tends to deter potential entrants because they can expect fewer sales. However, as this goodwill increases, the established firm tends to become fat and lazy, and this second effect encourages entry. The goodwill enjoyed by the established firm makes it reluctant to match price cuts by a new firm, so the entrant expects less competition. As Fudenberg and Tirole point out, firms may overinvest or underinvest in advertising, depending upon the relative strengths of these two effects. Advertising will not deter entry in those cases where the established firm is a fat-cat, and Fudenberg and Tirole provide several examples where established firms will advertise to *accommodate* entry rather than attempt to deter it. While overinvestment in advertising may deter entry in some cases, it will not always have this effect. This result weakens the case for general restrictions on advertising by firms since advertising does not always deter entry.

An interesting case where advertising can credibly deter entry has recently been developed by Baldani and Masson (1984). In their model demand depends solely upon advertising goodwill, and the firms' market shares are proportional to their share of industry goodwill. Since established firms can build up their stock of goodwill prior to entry, they can advertise to the point where no firms would want to enter the industry, even if the established firms stop advertising when entry takes place. Here the goodwill from previous periods will have lasting effects on demand into the future that discourage entry even if the established firm stops advertising now, and this acts as a binding commitment. From simulations of their model Baldani and Masson conclude that advertising can be an effective entry barrier.

While no one denies the possibility that advertising can deter entry in certain cases, it is not clear that the model presented by Baldani and Masson is general enough for policy recommendations. The point raised by Schmalensee (1983) and Fudenberg and Tirole (1984) is that entry deterrence with advertising is not as simple as earlier research suggested, and the Baldani and Masson model confirms this finding. Although the results obtained by Baldani and Masson are interesting, their model has several unusual features. For example, the assumption that demand is a function of goodwill shares does not follow from any received theories of consumer response to advertising. Consumers may respond to the goodwill accumulated by established firms individually, but no plausible models of consumer behavior suggest they respond to a firm's share of *industry* goodwill.

Another unusual feature of the model is that the incumbent firm can accumulate the desired level of goodwill prior to entry. If advertising goodwill accumulates slowly, entry deterrence with advertising will be more difficult since the incumbent firm may not be able to acquire the desired level of goodwill before the new firm enters the market. Furthermore, if the established firm is not certain when entry will occur, strategic deterrence becomes even more difficult. New firms may decide to enter an industry *more* rapidly to prevent the established firm from achieving its desired level of goodwill. This leads to strategic game considerations that Baldani and Masson overlook, and makes it possible that advertising *encourages* entry in the context of their model. Finally, advertising goodwill must be durable for their conclusions to hold. Although recent estimates by Ayanian (1983) support this conclusion, the results obtained by Ehrlich and Fisher (1982) and those presented in chapter 5 suggest that advertising does not have long-lived effects on demand. Again, these criticisms do not deny the possibility that advertising can deter entry, but they do suggest that deterrence with advertising is not easy to accomplish. Therefore, public policy to increase competition by limiting advertising expenditures should be developed cautiously.

Another line of argument has been developed recently in which economists have asserted that advertising by established firms may create barriers to entry by increasing rivals' costs. Salop and Scheffman (1983) and Rogerson (1984) have shown that it can be advantageous for a dominant firm in an industry to increase costs for all firms in the industry, even if this strategy affects the dominant firm's costs as much as rivals' costs. Cost-increasing strategies are often irreversible and therefore are more credible if all firms in the market are required to pay them. Dominant firms can accomplish this goal by imposing regulatory standards, product quality standards, or union wage contracts that affect all producers.

While it is clear that costs can be increased by the dominant firm in the previous examples, these authors also suggest that dominant firms can raise rivals' costs by increasing their advertising expenditures. Rogerson argues that this strategy will only be effective if entrants must match the advertising levels of the established firms. However, this is the crucial weakness in the argument. What economic mechanism requires potential entrants to match the advertising (or other) costs of the dominant firms? In the model developed by Baldani and Masson, market shares were proportional to the firms' shares of industry goodwill. This assumption requires entrants to increase their advertising whenever the established firm does so, but this assumption is arbitrary. No established theories of consumer demand suggest that consumers respond to a firm's share of industry goodwill. While such a response is conceivable, no models of optimal consumer choice have been developed along these lines.

A related problem with the argument concerns the effect of higher costs on the market. Salop and Scheffman (1983) and Rogerson (1984) all assume that increases in costs will only affect supply. This assumption is acceptable in cases where the increase in costs is due to government regulation, but it is not sensible in the case of advertising expenditures. If advertising outlays do not increase the demand for the product, why should firms advertise? One argument is that advertising merely allocates existing demand among the firms without changing total market demand. But why should consumers respond to advertising this way? If the dominant firm advertises excessively, what compels rival firms to advertise excessively as well? Taken to the extreme, why doesn't the dominant firm raise costs by digging ditches and filling them? If advertising by the dominant firm does raise rivals' costs, these models need some mechanism that creates incentives to ensure that rival firms match the outlays of the dominant firm. The mechanism is clear in the case of government regulation, but it is not at all clear with advertising. If advertising does not affect demand and does not make consumers better off, then there is no reason to assume that rival firms will match the advertising expenses of the dominant firm. Therefore it is not obvious that advertising can create entry barriers by raising rivals' costs. To support this argument a theory of consumer demand must be developed where consumers optimally respond to a firm's share of industry advertising; otherwise, some other mechanism is needed that requires rival firms to match the dominant firm's outlays. Without a mechanism to force rivals to match advertising expenses, it is unlikely that advertising can create entry barriers by raising costs.[15]

As a final note, even if rivals were forced to match the incumbent firm's advertising outlays, advertising is not the source of the entry barrier in these models. When a dominant firm is in a position to raise the costs of its rivals, any increase in costs that must be matched may deter entry. The barrier to entry exists because the established firm is a dominant firm (and therefore already has market power) and because rival firms are required to match the dominant firm's outlays. Advertising expenditures in such a case are merely symptoms of the problem, not the cause.

Other Issues Concerning Barriers to Entry

So far our discussion of entry barriers has emphasized the different definitions employed by Bain and Stigler. Recent work on the welfare effects of entry barriers points to broader considerations that are also important in the advertising/entry barrier debate, and we pursue these ideas in this section.

Economists object to entry barriers because they are considered to be inefficient. High profits indicate that output in an industry should increase and that more resources should be devoted to producing output in that market. Barriers to entry prevent these adjustments from occurring, which is inefficient and makes society worse off. However, recent work by Demsetz (1982), Fisher (1979), and von Weizsacker (1980) seriously challenges this view.

Demsetz argues that the notion of an entry barrier is far more vague than implied by the different definitions used by Bain and Stigler. After all, property rights are a barrier to entry created by our legal system. These rights prevent those who do not own assets from using society's resources. Economists do not consider property rights to be a barrier to competition because society's interests are best served by a property right system that creates "legal" barriers to competition. But this example makes clear the value judgments implicit in the barrier-to-entry approach. Property rights are not viewed as barriers to entry because they lead to outcomes that most economists view as efficient. Yet ownership rights prevent entry into an industry more effectively than advertising. Why should economists object to entry barriers in the latter case but not the former?

For example, many economists argue that advertising creates entry barriers because it allows firms to earn economic profits over time. But, as Demsetz notes, advertising is a legal property right, and it is not clear that society would benefit from limiting this right. In fact, Demsetz argues, if society limits property rights, these restrictions are likely to affect other markets (have "spillover effects") in addition to the market that is believed to be inefficient. For instance, legislation that restricts firms' property rights to advertise may cause concern among all property owners about their rights. This could cause a decline in property values and reduce incentives to work and invest. When cigarette firms were not allowed to advertise on television or radio, they found other means to achieve their goals (as did any consumers who may have relied on this advertising to guide their purchases). These reactions may have consequences that are worse than the initial inefficiency. Too often these spillover effects have been ignored in the debate over entry barriers.

Patents create legal barriers to entry which prevent competitors from using a technology without permission. The output of patented goods is lower than it would be if any firm could use the technology without restraint (if entry were "free"). Although society might prefer a higher rate of output of patented goods, a change that weakened the patent laws would also reduce the incentive to innovate. Society may be far worse off if less innovation occurs than if patent laws create a monopoly. If patent protection was not provided by the law, Demsetz argues, there would then be a barrier to innovation. Changes in property rights will clearly create new barriers to entry as surely as they reduce the old barriers.

The issues become more complex when there is uncertainty. Consider a firm that has an excellent credit rating which lowers its borrowing costs relative to a potential entrant. If the established firm earned higher profits as a result of its lower costs, there is a barrier to entry using Bain's definition. Yet, as Demsetz points out, a firm's credit history is an asset in a world of uncertainty where information is costly to obtain. The value of this asset is not likely to appear on the firm's balance sheet, so the accounting rate of return on assets will be higher than if this asset were capitalized. This might appear to be a barrier to entry, but society certainly does not want to discourage firms from obtaining good credit histories. Cheaper financing is not the barrier to competition; the barrier is the cost of acquiring information.

The same argument also applies to trademark protection. Without trademark protection firms would not develop products as fully as consumers would like because other firms could produce identical lower quality products. As Demsetz observes, our property right system encourages firms to seek long-term profits by granting legal protection to copyrights, patents, and trademarks. Without this legal protection, firms would be less inclined to invest in "permanence" and in long-term commitments. It may be efficient for society to encourage such permanence, even if competition is reduced. Conversely, it is not efficient to preserve competition at any cost nor is it efficient to reduce entry barriers at any cost. Legislators must take a much broader view of the costs and benefits of particular policy recommendations when trying to eliminate barriers to entry, or society may be worse off as a consequence.

Several of the points raised in the preceding paragraphs were developed separately by von Weizsacker (1980). He analyzed the welfare effects of barriers to entry within a specific model and developed an alternative definition of an entry barrier. According to von Weizsacker, a barrier to entry is a cost of producing which entrants must bear but is not borne by existing firms *and* which implies a distortion in the allocation of resources. In this respect his definition is an extension of Stigler's. To calculate the distortion in resource allocation, von Weizsacker considers what an omniscient planner might do to improve the situation and increase social welfare. This requires the planner to consider externalities which may arise from market operations, and emphasizes the broader context in which the entry barrier concept must be considered. From the simple models that he develops, von Weizsacker found that when there are economies of scale in production, several plausible cases exist where there are too *many* suppliers in equilibrium. In these cases, new firms should be prevented from entering the industry and existing firms should produce more output at a lower cost. These conclusions contradict those reached by the traditional view of economies of scale and entry barriers presented in the section "Economies of Scale in Advertising."

Similarly, in markets with differentiated products of varying quality, von Weizsacker finds that there are too few firms producing high-quality products, and too many producing low-quality products. This occurs because it is costly for consumers to determine whether a producer sells high- or low-quality goods. Because of information costs, new high-quality firms must sell their products at a discount until they earn a reputation in the market, and this reduces the number of high-quality firms. Despite the fact that the market outcome is not efficient in this model, von Weizsacker argues that there are no barriers to entry. The higher profits earned by high-quality firms who have obtained a reputation are needed to encourage new high-quality entrants. Since there are too few high-quality firms in the market, the inducement offered by higher profits is socially beneficial. The high profits earned by high-quality firms are not due to barriers to entry and do not indicate that these firms have monopoly power. The goodwill earned by these firms actually increases the efficiency of the market by reducing information costs; it is not a barrier to entry. These examples illustrate that what appear to be entry barriers in a partial equilibrium model are not inefficient in a more general framework. Again, care is required when making policy recommendations to eliminate these apparent barriers.

Conclusions

Several theories suggesting that advertising has anticompetitive effects have been analyzed in this chapter. Although the view of advertising as an entry barrier initially received support from earlier theoretical and empirical work, more recent research has seriously questioned this general conclusion. Economies of scale in advertising, once thought to be a source of entry barriers, are not measurable. Most research has shown that there are *diminishing* returns to advertising, indicating that advertising does not generally create cost advantages for larger firms. Even when consumers are more responsive to advertising by established brands, this is not an advantage created by advertising alone. Consumers may be more responsive because the established firm delivered the product first, or because the established firms have developed a valuable reputation for quality. In either case, advertising *alone* does not confer advantages to established firms. Therefore, advertising itself does not create entry barriers in these cases.

When established firms have first-move advantages, advertising can be used to deter entry. However, recent work has shown that advertising threats must be credible to deter entry and even then, credible entry deterrence with advertising is not a simple matter. Despite first-move advantages, established firms may find it optimal to pursue advertising policies that *accommodate* entry rather than deter it. Again, there is no general conclusion that advertising allows firms to reduce competition, although in certain cases it may have this result. Finally, recent literature on entry barriers has questioned the wisdom of a partial equilibrium approach to entry barriers. Policies that economists recommend to eliminate entry barriers may have important but unexpected consequences that may make society worse off. Therefore, it is crucial to identify the exact cause of the barrier to entry and to determine the likely costs and benefits from the policy change in a general equilibrium context. This argument suggests that the concept of barriers to entry is more ambiguous than many economists previously believed.

These remarks do not imply that advertising can never be a source of entry barriers. In specific cases advertising may seriously reduce competition. However, there is little support for the view that advertising *generally* reduces competition or that broad restrictions on all advertising by large firms will improve social welfare. The best recommendation at this point is a case-by-case approach. In those industries where advertising clearly has reduced competition, the profits of established firms should be raised above competitive levels, and this is a testable implication of the theory. When advertising by established firms causes increases in future profits, there is support for the hypothesis that advertising creates barriers to entry. However, since higher profits do not necessarily imply the existence of barriers to entry, economists must be careful to determine the source of the higher returns. When barriers to entry are responsible, some corrective actions may be justified if the social benefits from those actions are greater than the costs.

Notes

1. Comanor and Wilson (1974), p. 42.
2. This point has been raised several times by Simon (1965, 1970) and by Simon and Arndt (1983).
3. See Ornstein (1977), Ferguson (1974), and Comanor and Wilson (1979) for reviews of this literature.
4. Stigler (1983), p. 67.
5. See Demsetz (1982) and the discussion in "Other Issues Concerning Barriers to Entry."
6. See Varian (1978), p. 15.
7. See Comanor and Wilson (1979) and Simon (1980).
8. Established firms may have intertemporal advantages if they have the first move. See "Strategic Entry Deterrence with Advertising" and Salop (1979).
9. Although advertising goodwill does not affect the response of established firms to new entrants in this model, it can affect entry response in other models. See Schmalensee (1983), Fudenberg and Tirole (1984), and the section "Strategic Entry Deterrence with Advertising."
10. In fact, brand loyalty may reduce the power established firms have to prevent entry. See Fudenberg and Tirole (1984) and the discussion in "Strategic Entry Deterrence with Advertising."
11. In their criticism of Schmalensee's model, Comanor and Wilson do not consider the possibility that higher markups due to goodwill may not reflect economic profits. If the value of the goodwill were properly capitalized as an asset of the firm, reported profits would fall. See Demsetz (1979) and the discussion in chapter 4.
12. Fisher and McGowan (1983) have shown that accounting profit data provide little information about economic profits. See chapter 4.
13. This discussion is pursued in more detail in the section "Other Issues Concerning Barriers to Entry."
14. See Spence (1977) and Dixit (1980).
15. Nelson's (1974) model, discussed in the next chapter, does allow consumers to respond to the volume of advertising by a firm. However, in his model firms produce output which varies in quality, so the differences in advertising between firms reflect differences in quality. This is quite different from the case considered here, where the dominant firm simply raises its advertising volume.

3
Advertising, Risk, and Information

S everal of the theories reviewed in the previous chapter concluded that advertising reduces competition by creating barriers to entry. Advertising expenditures protected firms from competition and therefore raised profit rates. Proponents of this view predicted that advertising would be positively correlated with profit rates, and this prediction was confirmed by many cross-section studies of various industries in several countries. The hypothesis that advertising acts as a barrier to entry seemed to receive strong support from this evidence.

Despite the apparent support for the barrier-to-entry hypothesis, other interpretations of the evidence challenged this view. Several economists suggested that advertising might increase competition in markets, rather than reduce it, while others questioned whether the correlations truly supported the barrier-to-entry explanation. The major obstacle was to develop theoretical explanations that could account for the positive correlation between advertising and profits, and several theories that accomplish this task are presented in this chapter. All of the models emphasize the importance of risk and imperfect information in markets. In contrast to the models discussed in the previous chapter, these theories predict that advertising will not raise profits and may actually reduce them. This is a testable hypothesis which distinguishes the barrier-to-entry approach from the risk-information approach.

The effects of risk on the firm's advertising and pricing decisions are explored in the section "Advertising and Risk." In "Advertising as Information," Nelson's model emphasizing the role of imperfect information is discussed. A more general treatment of the role of information in markets has been developed recently by Ehrlich and Fisher (1982). Their model and related empirical results are presented in the section "Extensions of the Information Hypothesis," and concluding remarks follow.

Advertising and Risk

In their classic study, Dorfman and Steiner (1954) analyzed the optimal level of advertising for a monopolist. When the demand for the product depends upon its price and advertising expenditures, at the profit-maximizing level of advertising the marginal value product of advertising (μ) equals the negative of the price elasticity of demand (η). This result is easily derived from the profit-maximizing behavior of the firm. Consider the profit function for a monopolist when the demand curve, $Q(AP_a,P)$, depends upon the price of the product, P, and the level of the firm's advertising expenditures, AP_a:

$$\pi = Q(AP_a,P)P - C[Q(AP_a,P)] - AP_a, \tag{3.1}$$

where A is the number of advertising messages, P_a is the price of an advertising message, and $C(Q)$ is the firm's cost of production. Differentiating equation 3.1 with respect to advertising expenditures, AP_a, and setting the result equal to zero, we obtain the necessary first-order condition for a profit maximum:

$$\partial\pi/\partial AP_a = P\{\partial[Q(AP_a,P)]/\partial AP_a\}$$

$$- [dC(Q)/dQ][\partial Q(AP_a,P)/\partial AP_a] - 1 = 0 \tag{3.2}$$

Dividing both sides by $P[\partial Q(AP_a,P)]/\partial AP_a$ yields:

$$[P - dC(Q)/dQ]/P = (1/P)(\partial AP_a/\partial Q(AP_a,P)) = 1/\mu, \tag{3.3}$$

where $\mu = P\partial Q(A,P)/\partial AP_a$ is the marginal value product of advertising and $[P - dC(Q)/dQ]/P$ is the Lerner index of monopoly power, or the price–cost margin.

If we differentiate equation 3.1 with respect to price, P, we obtain

$$\partial\pi/\partial P = Q(AP_a,P) + P[\partial Q(AP_a,P)/\partial P]$$

$$- [dC(Q)/dQ][\partial Q(AP_a,P)/\partial P] = 0 \tag{3.4}$$

Rearranging equation 3.4 yields the familiar condition

$$[P - dC(Q)/dQ]/P = -1/\eta, \tag{3.5}$$

where $\eta = (\partial Q/\partial P)(P/Q)$. Equations 3.3 and 3.5 show that the monopolist will advertise where $-1/\eta = 1/\mu$. Combining equations 3.3 and 3.5 will yield the Dorfman–Steiner condition:

$$AP_a/PQ = \eta_a/-\eta, \tag{3.6}$$

where $\eta_a = (\partial A/\partial P)(A/Q)$ is the elasticity of demand with respect to advertising. This well-known condition states that a monopolist should set the advertising–sales ratio equal to the ratio of the advertising elasticity of demand divided by (the absolute value of) the price elasticity of demand to maximize profits.

Equation 3.5 can be used to illustrate the barrier-to-entry view of advertising. The arguments presented by Bain (1956) and by Comanor and Wilson (1979) suggest that advertising reduces the elasticity of demand for firms, which allows them to raise their prices over marginal cost and earn excess profits. Therefore the positive correlation between advertising and profits occurs because advertising reduces the elasticity of demand and this allows firms to increase their profits.

However, as equation 3.6 makes clear, the level of advertising itself depends upon the elasticity of demand. As the elasticity of demand falls, it is more profitable to advertise, so firms will increase their advertising expenditures. The positive relation between advertising and profits might occur because both variables respond to structural changes in the market, such as changes in the elasticity of demand. The correlation between advertising and profits does not establish a causal connection between the two variables. Does advertising cause profits to increase by reducing competition and the elasticity of demand? Or does advertising passively respond to changes in profits and the elasticity of demand? Those economists who disagree with the barrier-to-entry view of advertising generally assert that advertising responds to market conditions; it does not cause them to change.

For example, Horowitz (1970) found that when uncertainty is added to the profit-maximizing model, the optimal level of advertising is significantly affected by the manager's attitude toward risk. Furthermore, the manager's risk preferences have systematic effects on advertising decisions. Consider a firm in an industry where demand varies substantially from period to period, and where firms must produce output before they know the random level of demand. Horowitz showed that when unsold output must be scrapped, risk-averse managers will advertise more than is necessary to maximize the expected value of profits. Risk-averse managers advertise more to increase the probability of selling output that they have already produced, and this reduces the expected losses from unsold output.

The fluctuations in industry demand will also cause profits to vary, and variable profits will require a higher rate of return to compensate investors for greater risk. Therefore the uncertainty in the industry will tend to raise both advertising and profitability even without a causal connection between advertising and profits. This implies that the positive correlations discovered between advertising and profits may be misleading because risk-related variables have been omitted from previous studies. In the model developed by Horowitz, advertising, prices, and output are all determined simultaneously, and this implies that advertising expenditures cannot be considered exogenous in econometric studies.

Arguing along similar lines, Sherman and Tollison (1971, 1972) noted that the absolute value of the elasticity of demand also equals the inverse of Lerner's measure of monopoly power. Thus

$$P/(P - MC) = -\eta = \mu$$

or

$$(P - MC)/P = -1/\eta = 1/\mu, \tag{3.7}$$

where P is the product price, MC is the marginal cost of production, and $(P - MC)/P$ is the Lerner index of monopoly power (also known as the price–cost margin). They argued that the price–cost margin also reflects the technological properties of production; all else being equal, the lower the marginal (or variable) costs relative to total costs, the greater the price–cost margin. Since $\mu = P/(P - MC)$ in the Dorfman–Steiner model, higher values of the price–cost margin will be associated with lower values of the marginal value product of advertising. Assuming that the marginal value product of advertising is declining in the relevant range, this implies that lower values of μ will be associated with higher levels of advertising. As a result, a positive relation will be observed between the level of advertising and the price–cost margin, as many studies have discovered. However, the positive correlation between advertising and profits does not occur because advertising causes monopoly power; it simply reflects the technology of production.

Firms will advertise more when additional sales increase total profits, and this occurs when the short-run marginal cost, MC, is small relative to the price, P. Short-run marginal cost is likely to be small when fixed costs play an important role in production, and these high fixed costs will also lead to significant variations in profits over time. When fixed costs are large relative to marginal costs, each additional sale improves profits considerably, and this creates incentives for firms to advertise more to generate additional sales. Since profits will also vary considerably when demand varies and fixed costs are substantial, the firm's shareholders will demand higher returns to compensate for the greater risk. Therefore high levels of advertising will be observed with high profits because both are affected by the degree of cost variability.

The analysis presented by Sherman and Tollison suggests that advertising and profitability are positively related because researchers have omitted an important variable from their studies, the cost variability of production. When Sherman and Tollison added this variable to the profit equations used in previous work, the advertising–sales ratio did not significantly affect profits, and this result supported their position. They also found that the advertising–sales ratio was highly correlated with the cost–fixity variable, as predicted by the theory.

Sherman and Tollison's analysis also shows that the level of advertising is determined simultaneously with profitability, as shown in equation 3.7. This conclusion agrees with Horowitz's finding and implies that empirical researchers should not treat the level of advertising as an exogenous variable.[1] When advertising and profits are determined simultaneously, ordinary-least-squares estimates of the advertising–profits relation are biased. Many of the studies which discovered a positive relation between advertising and profits used ordinary least squares, so these results may be biased.

The models developed by Horowitz and Sherman and Tollison provide one possible explanation for the positive relation between advertising and profits: the systematic effects of profit-risk on firm behavior. In this light, the positive correlation observed between advertising and profitability provides less persuasive support for the barrier-to-entry hypothesis.

Advertising as Information

Many of the models developed to explore the effects of advertising in markets did not examine the behavior of consumers when information is incomplete and uncertainty is present. If all consumers had perfect information about product qualities, prices, and other relevant product characteristics, then advertising would be unnecessary. But when consumers are not perfectly informed, or when information is costly to obtain, advertising can play an important role in the market. In this section we will consider several theories that analyze advertising as a source of information.

Telser (1969) suggested a theory in which advertising supplies information to consumers in response to their demands. He argued that the equilibrium between the supply and demand for advertising would determine the total quantity provided. Nelson (1970, 1974) extended this approach and developed a formal model in which advertising supplies information to consumers about product quality and availability. Nelson argued that since advertising provides information to consumers (admittedly from a biased source), it is valuable to consumers and to society.

Advertising supplies information about a variety of product characteristics, including quality, sometimes price, and distribution outlets. When consumers are not completely informed, this information is crucial to improving their purchasing decisions. Consumers will use the information acquired through advertising along with other sources, such as search and word of mouth. Since advertising can be a less costly source of information to consumers than other sources, it is efficient to provide advertising messages. Advertising can also be the most cost-effective means for a firm to inform consumers about various product attributes. Therefore, Nelson asserts, advertising by firms allows society to use its resources efficiently.

How will advertising affect competition? Nelson reasons that the elasticity of demand depends upon the number of *known* alternatives. If a consumer is unaware of other brands or substitutes, then demand will be less responsive to price changes. Since advertising is a low-cost method of making consumers aware of substitute products, advertising can increase the elasticity of demand and improve competition in the market. Consumers cannot substitute brand X for brand Y if they are unaware that brand X exists. New firms can use advertising to make consumers aware of their products, and this increases competition and may increase the elasticity of demand. As Ferguson (1974) stressed, advertising can increase a firm's sales by informing consumers or by changing tastes. If advertising changes tastes, as the barrier-to-entry view asserts, then demand will become less elastic; if advertising informs consumers, demand may become more elastic.

If advertising does increase competition as Nelson claims, how do we explain the fact that advertising expenditures and profits are positively correlated? The answer, provided in Nelson's analysis, was expanded by Schmalensee (1976). To maximize profits, any firm will advertise until the marginal costs of advertising are equal to the anticipated marginal revenues. Those firms that are more efficient would benefit more from an incremental increase in sales than would firms that are less efficient. Since the more profitable firms have more to gain from increased sales, they will advertise more than the less profitable firms. Therefore advertising and profitability will be positively related, but not because advertising causes firms to be more profitable. The correlation between profitability and advertising is incidental.

Nelson's analysis indicates that advertising can increase competition and decrease prices despite the positive correlation observed between advertising levels and profits. Again, the key issue concerns the *causal* relation. Both the barrier-to-entry and information-risk theories can explain the correlation that is observed. However, the debate has focused on the causal mechanisms at work, and this is the crucial controversy in determining the effects of advertising on markets. Nelson's theory suggests that the correlations commonly used as proof that advertising is anticompetitive may be misleading. An alternative interpretation, where advertising promotes competition and increases efficiency, can fit the data equally well.

For example, consider the argument that advertising increases product differentiation and causes demand to become more inelastic. If the traditional interpretation is correct, then firms earn higher profits because they have manipulated consumer tastes, causing the elasticity of demand to fall. However, Nelson argues that if consumers have different tastes, there will be more product differentiation in the market anyway to accommodate the consumers' preferences. We should also observe more advertising as firms attempt to inform buyers about their specific brand to improve the "match" between product characteristics and the buyers' tastes. These results are the normal consequences of healthy competition in the market. From Nelson's perspective, firms differentiate their products and increase their advertising in an effort to satisfy consumer preferences, not to reduce competition. Therefore we would find more differentiation and advertising in a market in response to market forces and not because advertising alone differentiates the product. Advertising simply allows consumers to better select the brands that are more likely to appeal to them. This is an improvement over random consumer search, which is more costly, and it is also a less costly method for firms to inform potential customers about their products. Since advertising lowers the costs of acquiring and disseminating information, it increases efficiency even if competition is not increased.

Nelson's conclusion that advertising is efficient rests on the assumption that advertising is truthful. Why should advertising provide truthful information to consumers? Firms advertise to sell products, not to inform consumers. When will the selling job of advertising generate truthful information to consumers about product quality?

Nelson showed that in markets satisfying certain fairly weak requirements, it is in the firms' best interests to provide truthful advertising. To develop this argument Nelson divided goods into two categories: search goods and experience goods. Search goods are defined as those products whose quality can be easily determined by inspection. Once the consumer has seen the product, he or she can determine the verity of the advertising claims. In these markets firms must be truthful in their advertising since false claims are easily discovered. Consumers have considerable power over advertising statements in markets for search goods because these claims will be quickly tested before the consumer purchases the product. Under these constraints there is generally little benefit to the firm from false advertising, so Nelson argued that advertising will be truthful and informative in these markets because of the consumers' power.

Experience goods are those goods whose quality cannot be directly determined by the consumer before purchase. Consumers obviously exert less influence on advertising in these markets because the firm can earn profits in the short run even if advertising claims can be disproved. The problem with experience goods is that the consumer must buy them to determine if the advertising claims are truthful and even then they may be unable to disprove the claims. In these cases Nelson argued that the consumer has power over advertising only through repeat purchases. Nelson showed that advertising in experience-goods markets will be truthful if consumers believe that the truth of the statement does not raise profits from initial sales (versus repeat sales) or if the producer can make the advertising statement true at no cost. If either condition is satisfied, advertisements will be truthful and informative for experience goods as well.

The reputation of a firm also plays an important role in determining the truthfulness of advertising for both search and experience goods. Firms with established reputations have incentives to provide truthful advertising because they could easily sacrifice future sales and goodwill with false statements. Companies with established reputations have something to lose if they mislead their customers with false advertising, and so they are more likely to provide truthful information—even in markets for experience goods. This implies that consumers may be more willing to accept the advertising claims made by established firms since these firms have incentives to advertise truthfully. If this is true, then larger firms will tend to advertise more because customers are more willing to believe that their advertising is truthful, while smaller firms may have to use alternative and more personal methods to establish consumer trust.

When information is costly to obtain, firms must establish a reputation before consumers will fully trust their advertising. Until that time, their advertising will be less effective, and these companies must use more personal methods to sell their products (such as customer service, warranties, salespeople). This is not inefficient, and it does not imply that advertising reduces competition; it is simply a consequence of imperfect information. If large firms were prohibited from advertising, they would resort to other, less efficient ways to gain consumer confidence, and this could be costly to society. Certainly society does not want to implement policies that discourage investments in reputation and trust. Yet policies to restrict advertising by large firms may have precisely this effect.[2]

Nelson also argued that advertising may provide information to consumers even if the advertising message does not. In his theory the *volume* of advertising itself conveys information to consumers. Only the more efficient firms that are able to satisfy more customers on average can afford to advertise heavily. Therefore the level of advertising expenditures is an indirect signal of product quality in addition to the information content of that advertising. On average, the more efficient firms will advertise more heavily and the consumer should purchase those brands with the highest volume of advertising.

To test his theory, Nelson (1974) examined differences in the advertising–sales ratio between search and experience goods (as he classified the products) and durable versus nondurable goods. He argued that advertising expenditures should be greater for experience goods than for search goods and this prediction was supported by the test results. Nelson further asserted that the distribution of advertising expenditures by media will depend upon the search–experience distinction. Newspapers and magazines require more consumer attention than do television and radio. Therefore he predicted that search goods will advertise more frequently in newspapers and magazines because these media provide "hard," refutable information. Since information about experience goods is difficult to prove and verify, sellers of these goods offer more impressionistic advertising in the radio and television media. Nelson found overwhelming support for this prediction as well: all experience goods advertised more heavily in television compared with search goods. These tests offered strong evidence in favor of Nelson's theory of advertising.

Although Nelson's theory was supported by his tests, there are several weaknesses in the model. Ferguson (1974) criticized Nelson's theory because it explains differences in the advertising–sales ratio between search, experience, durable, and nondurable goods, but it does not describe differences in the advertising–sales ratio within these broad groups. Furthermore, the brand is the unit of analysis for Nelson, but he does not describe what determines the optimal number of brands in a market. Finally, the distinction between search and experience goods is *crucial* in Nelson's theory, yet the classification of products into these categories is somewhat arbitrary. This is an important criticism that can affect empirical tests of his theory.

Schmalensee (1978) showed that if advertising volume does provide indirect information about experience goods, then it could be inefficient for consumers to obey Nelson's rule and purchase those products that advertise more than others. In Schmalensee's model, simply buying those products that are more heavily advertised will not prevent less efficient producers from earning high profits. However, Kihlstrom and Riordan (1984) examined this issue more recently, and they found that Schmalensee's model was based on an *ad hoc* specification of consumer behavior. When consumer behavior was more properly modeled, Kihlstrom and Riordan found that Nelson's conclusions were upheld; advertising *volume* conveys information about product quality (acting as a "signal" of product quality to consumers of the good).

Albion and Farris (1981) criticized Nelson's approach because consumer preferences are fixed in his model and so advertising can affect *only* the information available; it cannot affect tastes. Since one of the goals of advertising is to change consumer tastes, they argue that Nelson's model is incomplete because it ignores this role. However, even if advertising changes consumer tastes, economists cannot directly test for this effect. And it is not possible to distinguish between a change in tastes and a change in the information set, so the "change-in-tastes" hypothesis does not provide testable restrictions. The information hypothesis, however, has several testable implications which *can* be refuted. Available evidence (which will be discussed in the section "Extensions of the Information Hypothesis") has not rejected the information theory. Finally, although it may be a goal of advertisers to change consumer tastes, that does not mean that advertising can effect such a change, nor does it imply that this is a role for advertising that economic theories must include. After raising this complaint, Albion and Farris themselves admit that we cannot distinguish between informative versus persuasive advertising and that the distinction is not fruitful.[3]

Despite these criticisms, Nelson's theory makes an important contribution by emphasizing the role of advertising as a source of information. If the theory is correct, advertising must be judged from a different perspective than the traditional analysis would suggest, and public policies to limit advertising must be carefully considered.

Extensions of the Information Hypothesis

Ehrlich and Fisher (1982) presented a model which extended Nelson's theory and stressed the importance of information in markets. They argued that too much emphasis has been placed by economists on the *effects* of advertising and too little on its determinants. They also agreed that the distinction between informative and persuasive advertising is not useful since persuasive advertisements can also be very informative. For example, advertising gimmicks which seem motivated by the intent to change tastes may actually make it easier for viewers to understand and remember the information presented. How, then, can we tell the difference between informative and persuasive advertising? Ehrlich and Fisher believe that we cannot distinguish between the two cases and that it is not productive to attempt such a distinction.

Their perspective is similar to Nelson's; advertising affects the demand for goods because it reduces the full price that the buyer pays for a product relative to the market price. When consumers do not have full knowledge about the characteristics of different products or brands, they incur information costs. These costs arise either from consumer search and time spent to acquire information about the product or from dissatisfaction with purchases because they did not meet the consumer's requirements. The full price, δ_{ij}, to the buyer, j, of any good, i, consists of the nominal price paid, P_i, *plus* these information (or transaction) costs. Ehrlich and Fisher assume that information costs consist primarily of the time lost as consumers gather information about the product and finally buy it. Thus the full price is

$$\delta_{ij} = P_i + w_j l_{ij}, \tag{3.8}$$

where l_{ij} measures the expected length of time spent per unit good, and w_j is the buyer's opportunity cost of time. The size of l will depend upon the total information available to the buyer about the good; the buyer's education and experience, as well as search; the information provided by media advertising, A; and other "selling services," e, supplied by firms. If a consumer has little experience with a product, or if the product is not heavily advertised, it will be more costly for the consumer to become informed about this purchase because he or she will have to devote more time to become informed.

Ehrlich and Fisher specify the "information production function" as follows:

$$l_{ij} = l_{ij}(A_i, e_i, K_{ij}, x_{ij}).\qquad(3.9)$$

This equation simply states that the length of time a consumer needs to acquire goods depends upon the level of advertising, A, other selling efforts, e, the education and experience of the buyer, K_{ij}, and the number of units purchased, x_{ij}. Presumably, the greater the buyer's education and the greater the number of units purchased, the lower the costs of acquiring information. Similarly, the greater the media advertising, A, and other selling services, e, the lower the costs of acquiring information. Therefore the function $l_{ij}(\cdot)$, the time spent by the buyer per unit of the good, is decreasing in all of these variables.

As the problem has been set up by Ehrlich and Fisher, buyers demand both products and information about them. This creates incentives for suppliers of products to supply information (through advertising, A, and selling efforts, e) if they can provide this information at a lower cost than the cost to the consumer from search. The optimal "mix" of consumer search and firm advertising will depend upon the product itself and the costs and benefits of supplying information about the good. That is, the level of advertising will depend upon the flow of information in the market and its cost. The optimal level of advertising does not depend upon rigid classifications of goods into search or experience categories. Instead, advertising expenditures will vary with the demand for and supply of information. Ehrlich and Fisher then proceed to develop the derived (consumer) demand for advertising and the firm's advertising supply function. If information is more costly for consumers to acquire than for firms to provide, consumers will benefit from advertising messages and will be willing to pay more for the product to cover the cost of advertising because their search costs will be reduced. Ehrlich and Fisher assert that advertising, price, profits, and sales are all jointly determined in the market.

If advertising increases, this will lower the full cost of acquiring the good (but not the nominal price paid for the product). Consumers may pay the same (or even a higher) price to acquire advertised products. However, the total costs of obtaining the good in terms of the time consumers spend learning about the products and their qualities plus the nominal price that they pay will fall. As a result, the conventional demand curve will shift out because the total cost of consuming the product has declined. We can show graphically the equilibrium that will result from the joint determination of advertising and market price. Consider the consumer's decision to purchase a product. The consumer can choose to get more information through search or he can rely on advertising information provided by the firm. If the firm charges a higher price, it will only be acceptable to buyers if offset by increased advertising (so that the full price to the consumer is constant). This effectively holds the utility level of the consumer constant, and we can derive

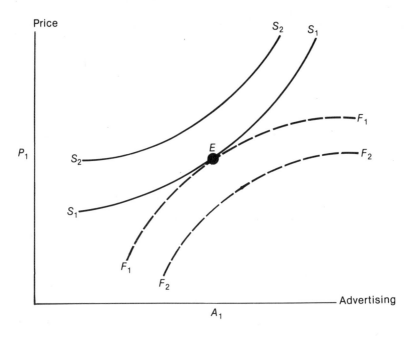

Note: Consumers are willing to pay a higher price only if the advertising expenditures reduce the full price of consumption. Utility is constant along the lines $F_1 F_1$. Profits for the firms are constant along the isoprofit lines $S_1 S_1$. Profits are constant if firms increase their advertising outlays when they increase price. Equilibrium is at point E with price P_1 and advertising level A_1.

Figure 3–1. Equilibrium Price and Advertising

"indifferrence" curves showing the trade-off between advertising and market price, keeping the utility level for the consumer constant.

In figure 3–1 these curves have positive slope and are concave to the origin (curves *FF* in the diagram), reflecting the fact that consumers are willing to pay higher *nominal* prices because information costs are reduced when advertising is increased. Along each indifference curve the consumer's utility (or well-being) remains constant. Curves to the right of $F_1 F_1$ represent higher levels of utility where the consumer is better off. This is intuitively plausible because curves to the right of $F_1 F_1$ provide more advertising at the same product price, or the same amount of advertising at a lower price. Either case represents an improvement in consumer welfare.

For the other side of the market, we can consider the firm's decision to "supply" advertising information. Holding profits constant, there will be a trade-off for the firm between higher product prices and advertising. If the firm increases the product's price, the same profit level can only be maintained by increasing advertising outlays. These "isoprofit" curves will have positive slope and are convex to the origin (curves SS). For the firm, curves to the left of $S_1 S_1$ represent higher profit levels since prices are higher with the same level of advertising or prices are the same but advertising expenditures are reduced. Either case represents higher profits for the firm.

Equilibrium in the market requires the consumers' indifference curves to be tangent to the firms' isoprofit curves. If the market for the good is competitive, then the equilibrium will occur where the firms earn zero economic profits. Zero economic profits are earned because of competition between producers to supply the good to consumers at the lowest "full price." If the firm is a monopolist, advertising, product price, and profits will be affected by market conditions in addition to the monopolist's costs. The zero profit curve would then be replaced by a set of isoprofit curves where the monopolist would attempt to reach the highest level of profits given consumer preferences. Even in the monopoly case, the equilibrium level of advertising will minimize the information costs to the consumer since this allows the monopolist to earn the highest level of profits. So in Ehrlich and Fisher's model, advertising levels are efficient whether the market is monopolized or perfectly competitive, and in both cases, advertising, price, and profits are all determined simultaneously in the market.

The theory of advertising presented by Ehrlich and Fisher improves upon Nelson's analysis in several important respects. First, they emphasize the importance of time and information costs in addition to the nominal price charged to buyers. These costs are not directly measurable yet they have a significant impact on the market equilibrium. For example, if economists found identical products selling at different prices in a market, they might conclude there is insufficient competition. However, the model developed by Ehrlich and Fisher suggests that the price differentials we observe may be due to differences in the information and time costs to the buyer. Since advertising reduces the time cost of consumption in their theory, some consumers are willing to pay a higher nominal price for advertised products, all else being equal (as illustrated in figure 3–1). The traditional view would assert that advertising reduces the elasticity of demand and causes higher prices because competition is reduced. The alternative view is that advertising provides a service to consumers which they are willing to pay to receive.

Nelson's theory did not explain differences in advertising intensities within broad product groups, such as between two search goods or two experience goods, but Ehrlich and Fisher's model does provide testable hypotheses regarding advertising levels within broad product groups. They argue that advertising will vary with the value of time to the customer; products that are sold to high-income groups should be advertised more than products sold to lower income groups, *ceteris paribus*. Therefore airline travel, which is typically consumed by people with high incomes, should be advertised more than substitutes for air travel that are consumed by lower income groups, such as railways or buses. Products with considerable mass appeal will be advertised more than products that appeal only to smaller groups, all else being equal, because media advertising for mass products is likely to be less costly and more productive than consumer search for these goods.

Advertising intensity will also vary between products because of differences in the costs to the firms of supplying advertising messages. Producer goods, for example, are sold to a more identifiable and knowledgeable group than consumer goods. As a result, the "marginal productivity" of other selling efforts, such as trade shows and exhibitions, will be greater than more general media advertising for producer goods. Therefore Ehrlich and Fisher predict proportionally less media advertising for these goods than for consumer goods.

To test their model, Ehrlich and Fisher regressed advertising intensity, measured as the log of real advertising expenditures by industry, against the logarithms of real industry sales, the relative price of advertising messages, the real hourly wage rate, and employment. The industry groups were roughly the same as the one- and two-digit Standard Industrial Classifications. The theory predicts that the level of real advertising should be positively related to the level of real sales, the real hourly wage rate, and the employment level since these variables reflect the value of time to consumers and the productivity of advertising to the firm. The relative price of advertising should have a negative impact on real advertising expenditures, as conventional demand theory would predict. The results confirmed these predictions in virtually every industry group tested, offering strong support for their model.

Another important point should be noted about the empirical results obtained by Ehrlich and Fisher. The barrier-to-entry view of advertising does not predict that the real hourly wage rate will have any impact on advertising expenditures by firms. However, the consumer information model developed by Ehrlich and Fisher does predict that advertising will increase as real wages increase. According to the information theory, the value of time to consumers will affect their willingness to search for products and their demand for advertising. As income rises, consumers will be less willing to spend time searching for information about a product (because their time is more valuable), and they will be more willing to pay for advertising which provides this information to them. Therefore the significant, positive coefficient on real hourly wages provides strong support for the information theory of advertising because the alternative theory predicts that this variable should have no effect on advertising.

Ehrlich and Fisher also obtained interesting results regarding the duration of the effects of advertising. They included a variable measuring the "stock" of advertising to reflect the possibility that past advertising expenditures could affect the current market equilibrium. They discovered that all advertising expenditures were fully depreciated within the year. That is, advertising had *no* durable effects on sales beyond the current year. However, their model does allow for a typical "life-cycle" pattern of advertising. Even though advertising effects may not be durable, consumer knowledge of a product can be durable within this framework. Initial advertising tends to be very productive if consumers do not know about the product (such as when a new product is introduced), but after a period of time, the productivity of these expenditures will decline (as the product matures) because most consumers will be aware of it.

The model developed by Ehrlich and Fisher offers considerable explanatory power in analyzing and testing the effects of advertising. Their theory is more flexible than Nelson's because advertised products are not rigidly classified as search or experience goods. Rather, advertising intensity and effectiveness will vary with changes in the market.

A recent study by Caves and Williamson (1985) provided additional support for the risk and information theories reviewed in this chapter. They argued that two general models were theoretically sufficient to explain product differentiation (which they define as occurring in markets where there are several producers, each facing a negatively sloped demand curve). One explanation, the product-attribute model, asserts that product varieties do not often match consumer preferences. When the product is inherently complex and there are fixed costs of producing each variety, firms cannot supply an infinite variety of products to satisfy each buyer's tastes. Therefore only a small number of brands will be produced in the market, and they will be imperfect substitutes for each other in the eyes of consumers. If one firm changes the price of its product, it will cause some consumers to switch brands, yielding a negatively sloped demand curve for each firm.

The information-based model of product differentiation asserts that consumers are not completely informed and therefore select a portfolio of information sources (advertising, opinions, search) to guide their purchases. Since buyers have different information sets, they purchase different brands for any set of prices even if their preferences are identical. When the price of one product changes, some buyers will switch brands and therefore the firm will observe a negatively sloped demand curve for its product.

Although these two models do not exhaust the possible sources of product differentiation, Caves and Williamson argue that many observable market conditions can be explained by these two theories. To test this assertion, Caves and Williamson, used canonical factor analysis with industry data from the United States and Australian manufacturing industries. The variables in the study were:

* infrequent purchases (the proportion of industry products which the buyer purchases once a year or less often);

* media advertising measured by the advertising–sales ratio;

* total selling expenses net of media outlays (as a percentage of total sales);

* the proportion of products where marketing efforts focus on intermediate sellers instead of the final user;

** proportion of industry products manufactured to buyers' specifications;

** proportion of products requiring moderate to high sales or technical service;

** proportion of products that are not a major purchase for the buyer;

** research and development outlays as a percentage of sales.

Those variables with one asterisk (*) above reflect the information-based sources of product differentiation since they measure the flow of information in the market from seller to buyer. Caves and Williamson found that media outlays were not a significant *independent* measure of product differentiation, but were important when combined with other selling expenses. It appears that these two sources of advertising expense are substitutes for one another, as suggested by Ehrlich and Fisher's model.

Those variables with two asterisks (**) reflect aspects of the product-attribute model, such as the scope for innovation through research and development and the degree to which the product is customized or mass-produced. This factor reflects the cost-fixity effect, emphasized by Sherman and Tollison (1972), in addition to other factors. Once again, Caves and Williamson found strong support for this theory of product differentiation. The two theories together were able to account for most of the variation in the data.

These results suggest that much of the variation in industry advertising occurs because of the structure of information flows in the industry. Advertising intensity is high when buyers have poor information or when producers cannot inform consumers through other means. Producers do not appear to advertise heavily simply to create barriers to entry; they advertise in response to the flow of information in the market and in response to product attributes. Many previous studies employed the advertising–sales ratio as a measure of product differentiation—a structural feature of markets—without recognizing that the level of advertising is determined by market structure.[4] The models discussed in this chapter all emphasize that advertising is determined by market structure, and the results obtained by Caves and Williamson support this interpretation.

Conclusions

In this chapter we have reviewed theories that offer alternative explanations of the positive correlation between advertising and profitability. In contrast to the theories discussed in chapter 2, these models emphasize the role of uncertainty in markets. Horowitz (1970) and Sherman and Tollison (1971, 1972) modeled the effects of risk on firm behavior and argued that the correlation between advertising and profits has been observed because important risk-related variables have been omitted in empirical research. These theories stress that advertising outlays will be affected by a structural feature in the market: the level of risk as measured by the variability of profits.

Telser (1969, 1978), Nelson (1970, 1974), and Ehrlich and Fisher (1982) assert that advertising enhances competition by providing information. These models emphasize that advertising decisions will be affected by the information structure of the industry. They also provide testable hypotheses that have been confirmed by empirical research. Overall there is strong support for the view that advertising responds to the structure of the market. This interpretation has been confirmed by Caves and Williamson (1985) in their study of the sources of product differentiation.

The positive correlation between advertising and profits is no longer sufficient to prove that advertising reduces competition. In this chapter alternative explanations of the role of advertising have been discussed and the testable restrictions of these models have been stressed. If advertising increases competition or simply responds to risk, then the elasticity of demand and profits will either fall or remain unchanged by current advertising. If advertising reduces competition, then the elasticity of demand should be reduced and future profits should be increased by current outlays. These are the implications of the two competing views of advertising and competition, and they will be tested in chapter 5. However, we must consider some important measurement and methodological problems before implementing the causal tests, and these issues are discussed in the next chapter.

Notes

1. Schmalensee (1972) showed that advertising was not an exogenous variable and warned against using ordinary least squares to estimate advertising equations. Yet researchers persist in assuming that advertising is exogenous.

2. Demsetz (1982) raises a similar argument in a different context. See chapter 2.

3. Albion and Farris (1981), p. 38.

4. This criticism was also raised by Sherman and Tollison (1972).

4
Measurement Issues and Methodology

From the discussion in the two preceding chapters it is clear that the causal relation between advertising and profitability (or market power) is one of the crucial issues in the advertising controversy. The empirical research undertaken to date has not shed much light on this important question. In this chapter we will discuss the difficulties that arise in measuring and testing the advertising–profits relation as well as the solutions proposed in this study.

Recent work by Fisher and McGowan (1983) has shown that the accounting rate of return is a poor measure of the economic rate of return. Therefore the first two sections of the chapter address the problem of correctly measuring profitability and market power for empirical work and the implications of using these measures for the tests in chapter 5. In the third section, "Measuring Advertising Intensity," we consider appropriate measures of advertising intensity. Conclusions follow in the final section of the chapter.

Measuring Profitability

As mentioned previously in chapter 2, economic theory asserts that in long-run competitive equilibrium the returns earned by marginal investments should be equal across industries after adjusting for risk. If investors are able to earn higher returns in some industries, then capital will leave industries with lower marginal returns, and move into industries with higher marginal returns. As Fisher (1984) has emphasized, the internal rate of return on the marginal investment is the signal for the entry and exit of resources. When an industry is not competitive and firms are protected by barriers to entry, the risk-adjusted return earned by that industry, at the margin, should exceed the returns earned elsewhere. Persistently high economic returns in an industry are a signal of monopoly power.

The accounting rate of return (measured as current profits divided by equity or total assets) has often been used as a measure of the economic rate of return. Industries with above-average accounting rates of return were presumed to have above-average economic rates of return and this indicated the presence of entry barriers. However, accounting profits have been criticized as a measure of economic profits because many assets are not properly valued (capitalized) on the balance sheet by conventional accounting procedures. For example, Telser (1969), Peles (1971), Bloch (1974, 1980), Demsetz (1979), and Ayanian (1975, 1983) have argued that advertising creates goodwill, which is a valuable asset to the firm. If advertising does create durable goodwill, then expenditures on advertising would be similar to investments in durable assets. However, accountants treat advertising as a current expense, not as an investment, and this may cause an upward bias in the accounting rate of return.

Advertising increases the accounting rate of return because the value of the goodwill created by advertising is not added to the firm's assets. If advertising goodwill were added to the firm's assets, the accounting rate of return on assets would be lower since a larger asset value would be divided into the same level of net income. Therefore advertising would be correlated with high accounting profits because the value of the firm is systematically understated when firms advertise.

The upward bias in accounting profits will increase as advertising expenditures increase (relative to the growth rate of the firm), and as the durability of advertising capital (goodwill) increases. Clearly this bias could account for the positive correlation between advertising and profits. If advertising expenditures were treated as an investment, recorded accounting profits would be lower. Demsetz (1979) found support for this view and asserted that the positive correlation between advertising and profits is simply an artifact of accounting techniques. Several researchers have attempted to correct reported profit rates by capitalizing industry advertising expenditures.[1] However, the results from these studies were sensitive to the depreciation rate used to amortize the advertising capital.[2]

Further examination of this research would not be useful though, since a far more serious criticism of the accounting rate of return has been raised by Fisher and McGowan (1983). They argued that the accounting rate of return reflects monopoly power only to the extent that accounting returns measure economic returns. In most situations, Fisher and McGowan asserted, the accounting rate of return is a poor and potentially misleading measure of the economic rate of return.

To prove their position, Fisher and McGowan developed a theoretical model in which they compared the economic rate of return with the accounting rate of return. They found that changes in the firm's growth rate, its depreciation rate, and the time pattern of future earnings from investments would cause the accounting rate of return to diverge from the economic rate of return. Only in one very unrealistic case would the accounting rate of return equal the economic rate of return. Fisher and McGowan simulated a model of a firm whose economic rate of return was known to determine the size of the discrepancy between accounting rates of return and the economic rate of return. They then examined the accuracy of the accounting rate of return as a measure of the economic return while changing the firm's growth rate and the "time shape" of future earnings from current investment. These simulations showed that the errors from using the accounting rate of return as a proxy for the economic return could be substantial. Therefore Fisher and McGowan concluded that accounting rates of return provide very little information about economic rates of return.

Why are accounting rates of return such poor measures of the economic rate of return? As Fisher noted, the problem is not simply that accounting profits are an imperfect measure of economic profits. It is true that accounting practices do not correctly capitalize certain activities such as advertising or research and development, and they do not adequately treat the problem of asset valuation in periods of inflation. However, even when these difficulties are ignored, accounting measures still do not accurately reflect economic returns. The problem is simply this: the economic rate of return on current investment is based upon the profit stream that an investment generates over its lifetime, now and into the future. To calculate the economic rate of return we must link the revenues earned with the specific investments that generated them. The accounting rate of return relates current profits to *all* investments owned by the company (total assets), including those assets that did not contribute to current profits. If a firm buys a new machine whose operating costs in the first year exceed the revenues it earns, the economic return on that investment is negative for that year. Yet the accounting rate of return averages net income over all assets, as though the new machine made a contribution to current profits, so the accounting rate of return does not link the net profits earned with the specific investments that generated those profits. Since the accounting rate of return relates current profits to all current capital, it fails to reflect the specific returns to each investment as required by economic theory, and as a result, it misstates the economic rate of return.

As van Breda (1984) and Fisher (1984) emphasize, the crucial problem is not simply that the accounting rate of return misstates the economic return, but that the direction of the bias is unknown unless the time pattern of net benefits produced by investments is known. Economists do not have enough information to determine the time shape of benefits produced by investments, so the economic rate of return cannot be calculated. Yet it is the economic rate of return, the expectation of future profits, that signals whether resources should flow toward one industry or another. Since the accounting rate of return changes with the time pattern of future earnings, it will deviate from the economic rate of return whenever the time shape varies. Unless economists know the time pattern of profits earned by investments, they cannot determine how the accounting rate of return will deviate from the economic rate of return. The accounting rate of return may exceed, equal, or be less than the economic rate of return depending upon the time pattern of profits. If the time pattern is unknown, accounting returns provide little information about the economic rate of return. When the time pattern of benefits is known, the economic return can be calculated directly, and accounting returns are not needed.

Fisher and McGowan's (1983) criticism of accounting profits creates a major problem for those researchers who have used accounting rates of return as a substitute for the economic rate of return. Virtually all of the studies relating advertising and profitability have used the accounting rate of return or the rate of return on sales as a measure of economic profits, so the results of these studies are now very much in doubt.

Long and Ravenscraft (1984) criticized Fisher and McGowan's conclusions and attempted to show that in practice, accounting profits are correlated with economic profits. However, their evidence was indirect (as it must be since the economic rate of return is not known) and inconclusive. In his reply to Long and Ravenscraft, Fisher (1984) argued that we should expect accounting rates of return to be correlated with economic rates of return. But even if the correlation is high, the accounting rate of return will be an imperfect measure of the economic rate of return. More important, when researchers use accounting rates of return as a proxy for the economic rate of return, they will introduce measurement errors into their studies, and Fisher argues that these measurement errors will often be correlated with the other variables used to explain profitability in statistical research. If this occurs, then even in cases when the measurement error from accounting profits is small (that is, when accounting profits are a good proxy for economic profits), the estimates obtained with accounting profit data will be biased.[3] Those who wish to use accounting profit data must show that accounting profits are a good proxy for economic profits *and* that the measurement error is not correlated with other variables in the model. Otherwise, an alternative measure of economic profits (or monopoly power) is needed that avoids the Fisher and McGowan criticism.

An Alternative Measure of Market Power

In the previous section we found that high accounting rates of return do not necessarily indicate the presence of monopoly power. Since the crucial issue in the advertising debate concerns the effects of advertising on monopoly power, it is important to find some observable measure of market power.

Martin (1985) has suggested a useful approach to measuring market power, which is discussed in this section.

Martin argues that the critical issue is not how the rate of return should be measured, but how market power, if it exists, will affect the rate of return. To see this, consider a firm producing in an oligopoly where all firms charge the same price for their product. Although this is a simplification of Martin's model, it is sufficient to illustrate his approach and the issues involved. The market price, p, is a function of industry output, Q, (or $p = f[Q]$). Industry output is simply the sum of the output produced by each firm in the industry, q_i, thus $Q = \Sigma q_i$. The profit function for each firm is:

$$\pi_i = f(Q)q_i - C_i(q_i) \tag{4.1}$$

where $C_i(q_i)$ is the i-th firm's cost of production.

Each firm maximizes profits by selecting its output level. To find the optimal level of output for the i-th firm, differentiate equation 4.1 with respect to the i-th firm's output:

$$d\pi_i / dq_i = p + q_i(dp/dQ)(dQ/dq_i) - C_i = 0, \tag{4.2}$$

where $C_i = dC_i(q_i)/dq_i$. Rearranging equation 4.2 yields

$$(p - C_i)/p = -(q_i/p)(dp/dQ)(dQ/dq_i). \tag{4.3}$$

If we define the i-th firm's market share, s_i, as q_i/Q, then equation 4.3 becomes:

$$(p - C_i)/p = -[s_i(Q/p)](dQ/dp)(dQ/dq_i)$$

or,

$$(p - C_i)/p = (s_i/\eta)(dQ/dq_i), \tag{4.4}$$

where η is the absolute value of the industry elasticity of demand.

The output for the industry, Q, consists of the output of the i-th firm, q_i, plus the output of all the other firms in the industry, Q_o, by definition. Therefore, the last derivative on the right-hand side of equation 4.4 can be written as:

$$dQ/dq_i = dq_i/dq_i + dQ_o/dq_i = 1 + \alpha_i,$$

where α_i is the i-th firm's belief about how the output of the other firms in the industry will respond to a change in its output. The term α_i is often called the conjectural variation of the i-th firm. If we do not restrict how the i-th firm's conjectures are formed, then equation 4.4 is simply:

$$(p - C_i)/p = [s_i(1 + \alpha_i)]/\eta \qquad (4.5)$$

The left-hand side of equation 4.5 is the Lerner index of monopoly power. Since competition forces firms to charge a price equal to marginal cost, firms have greater monopoly power the greater the difference between the price they charge and the marginal cost of production. Economists do not generally observe a firm's marginal costs, so it is often assumed that average costs are equal to marginal costs in the relevant range (a somewhat restrictive assumption, but necessary to make the Lerner measure operational). If this assumption is made, multiplying the left-hand side of equation 4.5 by output, q_i, will yield the rate of return on sales. Martin (1984) and Long and Ravenscraft (1984) suggested that this measure of profitability can be used as a measure of monopoly power to avoid the problems with accounting rates of return.

Unfortunately, Fisher (1986) showed that the rate of return on sales is not an accurate measure of the Lerner index of monopoly power. In fact, the profit–sales ratio fails to measure the Lerner index for the same reasons that the accounting rate of return fails to measure economic returns. As Fisher notes, the basic problem is that the Lerner index requires measurement of the firm's marginal cost of production, which includes the marginal cost of capital. This requires an accurate measure of the economic cost of capital, but the economic cost of capital depends upon the time shape of real benefits generated by investments. As in the case with the accounting rate of return, accounting practices regarding depreciation costs and the opportunity cost of capital do not meet the requirements of economic theory. Fisher shows that the profits–sales ratio will not equal the Lerner measure in general, and simulations revealed that the errors from using this ratio can be large. Therefore the profit–sales ratio cannot generally be used as a measure of monopoly power.

However, equation 4.5 can be manipulated to determine how market power might affect the return on sales, and Martin (1985) pursues this route. Adding and subtracting average cost (AC) on the left hand side of equation 4.5 will yield (after rearranging):

$$(p - AC)/p = [s_i(1 + \alpha_i)]/\eta + (MC - AC)/p \qquad (4.6)$$

or

$$(p - AC)/p = [s_i(1 + \alpha_i)]/\eta + [(MC/AC) - 1](AC/P) \qquad (4.7)$$

The ratio of marginal cost to average cost in the brackets above measures the importance of economies of scale in production. If costs are declining in the relevant range, then average cost will exceed marginal cost. The greater the decline in costs as output rises, the smaller is the (MC/AC) term in equation 4.7, and this reduces the price-average cost margin.[4]

One final step is required to obtain the result needed for this study. As a general rule, each firm in an industry does not advertise to change the elasticity of industry demand—it advertises to change the elasticity of demand only for its product (unless there is strong collusion in the industry). Needham (1976) provides a link between the elasticity of demand for the firm and the elasticity of demand for the market in a model such as this. The elasticity of demand for the market is defined as:

$$\eta = -(dQ/dp)(p/Q) = -[(dQ_o + dq_i)/dp](p/Q) \qquad (4.8)$$

which yields (after rearranging):

$$\eta = \eta_i s_i + \eta_o s_o, \qquad (4.9)$$

where $\eta_o = -(dQ_o/dp)(p/Q_o)$ is the elasticity of demand faced by all the other firms in the market, and $s_o = Q_o/Q$ is the market share of the other firms in the market. Thus the market elasticity of demand is equal to the i-th firm's elasticity of demand multiplied by its market share, plus the elasticity of demand for the other firms multiplied by their market share. Substitution into equation 4.7 then produces:

$$(p - AC)/p = [s_i(1 + \alpha_i)]/(\eta_i s_i + \eta_o s_o) \qquad (4.10)$$
$$+ [(MC/AC) - 1](AC/p)$$

Multiplying and dividing the left hand side by q_i yields:

$$(pq_i - TC)/pq_i = [s_i(1 + \alpha_i)]/(\eta_i s_i + \eta_o s_o) \qquad (4.11)$$
$$+ [(MC/AC) - 1](AC/p),$$

where TC is the firm's total cost of production ($TC = [AC]q_i$).

What are the effects of market power on the returns earned by this firm? If the market is competitive, then the elasticity of demand faced by the i-th firm is infinite and its market share will not affect the return on sales in equation 4.11 above. However, if the firm does have market power, Martin argues, the market share of the i-th firm will significantly affect the return on sales after controlling for economies of scale and average costs. This is the observable effect of market power on the firm's rate of return, and economists can test for the significance of the market share variable. Economists cannot estimate equation 4.11 as it stands because costs appear on both sides of the equation (multiplying and dividing the right-hand side of equation 4.11 by q_i will cause total costs per unit of sales to appear on both sides of the equation). However, it is not necessary to estimate equation 4.11 to test for the effects of advertising on competition (although Martin does offer suggestions regarding the estimation of equation 4.11).

Martin (1985) extends this model in several important respects, but the important relationships needed for this study have been established. If advertising increases market power, it may do so by reducing the firm's elasticity of demand, increasing its market share, or both. These changes will raise the return on sales earned by that firm. Therefore if advertising increases market power, all else being equal, it must cause an increase in the rate of return on sales. This should be the observable consequence of an increase in market power caused by advertising. Although Fisher (1986) is correct in arguing that the rate of return on sales is not an accurate measure of the Lerner index of monopoly power, it is nonetheless true that the rate of return on sales should increase, all else being equal, if advertising reduces competition. This is the hypothesis tested in this study, and further details regarding the econometric tests (such as omitted variables problems and other sources of bias suggested by Martin (1985) and by Fisher (1986)) are provided in chapter 5.

Measuring Advertising Intensity

Thus far the discussion of the advertising debate has implicitly assumed that, whatever the potential effects, advertising expenditures can be accurately measured. But there is some disagreement among economists and marketing professionals concerning the proper measurement of this variable. Basically, the problem concerns two issues:

1. What specific expenditures should be considered as advertising? As Albion and Farris (1981) have noted, the answer is not entirely clear. Are demonstration products considered an advertising expenditure? Free samples?

2. How should researchers measure advertising intensity? Most economic studies have employed the advertising–sales ratio as a measure of industry advertising intensity. However, some economists have also used the log of advertising expenditures in empirical research, and others have measured the number of advertising messages viewed by the public. Which of these measures is appropriate?

Regarding the first issue, firms often include other selling expenses in addition to advertising costs when they calculate total expenditures on advertising. Unfortunately, many expenses that are generally not considered to be sales-related are often included in these figures (such as overhead costs). Worse, firms are not consistent in the way they classify selling expenses; some firms include free goods or rebates in the advertising budget while others do not.[5] Because practices vary between firms and over time, there are substantial variations in the total advertising expenses reported by each firm which have nothing to do with changes in marketing efforts. For these reasons, total advertising expenditures can be a misleading measure of advertising outlays.

Since total advertising expenditures are not measured accurately, only advertising expenditures in specific media are considered in this study. These expenditures are measured accurately and consistently over the sample period, so changes in these expenditures are more likely to reflect changes in marketing strategy. Although other selling expenses represent an important aspect of marketing strategy and are a useful source of information in Ehrlich and Fisher's model (discussed in chapter 3), many important issues in the advertising debate can be analyzed excluding these costs. For example, public policy toward advertising has been concerned with media advertising and not with other selling expenses. Legislated bans and restrictions, such as those applied to the cigarette and alcoholic beverages industries, have been directed at media advertising and not at other selling expenses. Similarly, the controversy surrounding the effects of advertising on competition has focused primarily on media advertising by large firms. Therefore, as a result of data limitations and policy interest, our investigation will focus on advertising expenditures in specific media, even though this measure does not reflect all of the important elements in the total advertising budget.

Advertising intensity is also difficult to measure. The advertising–sales ratio arises quite naturally out of the profit-maximization problem of the firm, so this measure has been frequently employed. Consider again the case of a monopolist facing the demand curve $Q(P, AP_a)$ presented in chapter 3. The profit function for the firm is:

$$\pi = Q(P, AP_a)P - C[Q(P, AP_a)] - AP_a, \qquad (4.12)$$

where, again, A represents the level of advertising messages, P_a is the price of advertising messages, and P is the product price. As in chapter 3, differentiating the profit function with respect to advertising expenditures, AP_a, and setting the result equal to zero will yield the necessary first-order condition for the optimal level of advertising expenditures. From this result (equation 3.2 in chapter 3), if we define the advertising elasticity of demand, $\eta_a = (\partial Q / \partial AP_a)(AP_a / Q)$, and rearrange that equation, we obtain the following result:

$$AP_a/PQ = \eta_a[P - dC(Q)/dQ]/P \qquad (4.13)$$

or,

$$AP_a/PQ = \eta_a/-\eta, \qquad (4.13')$$

which is the Dorfman–Steiner condition. Equations 4.13 and 4.13' simply show that the advertising–sales ratio can be related to the price–cost margin or to the ratio of the advertising elasticity of demand divided by the normal-price elasticity of demand. From these results it seemed natural for economists to use the advertising–sales ratio as a measure of advertising intensity.

It would appear from the Dorfman–Steiner model that the advertising–sales ratio is an acceptable measure of advertising intensity, but this does not imply it is theoretically correct. The notation used in the model obscures a crucial point: does demand respond to the total advertising budget? Intuitively it should be clear it does not. Firms cannot simply spend money on advertising and expect that act alone to affect market demand. All else equal, the greater the number of potential customers exposed to an advertising message, the greater the response in demand. The volume of messages observed by potential customers is a crucial aspect of advertising which affects the demand for a product, not simply the total dollars spent or the ratio of advertising to sales. After all, consumers must see an advertisment to be affected by it.

According to the notation in the Dorfman–Steiner model, demand is a function of the product price and advertising expenditures, AP_a. This functional relation is incorrect given the preceding argument. Demand is not affected by total advertising expenditures, but by the number of messages observed by potential customers. Therefore advertising expenditures must be deflated by a price index for advertising that measures changes in the cost of advertising per number of viewers. Deflating total advertising expenditures by this index will provide a measure of real advertising expenditures made by the firm (the number of messages per potantial buyer).

Although this measure of advertising intensity has been used by Schmalensee (1972) and by Ehrlich and Fisher (1982), most researchers continue to use the advertising–sales ratio as a measure of advertising intensity. Since it is only by coincidence that the price of advertising messages per potential viewer will change by exactly the same amount as the change in the product price, the advertising–sales ratio cannot accurately measure advertising intensity. In fact, no theories of consumer behavior suggest that buyers respond to the ratio of advertising to sales or to total advertising expenditures. However, several theories demonstrate that consumer demand will respond to changes in the number of advertising messages received by potential customers.[6] The demand function is properly specified when the number of advertising messages viewed by the public is included, not simply the total number of advertising dollars spent, the log of total expenditures, or the ratio of advertising to sales. The number of advertising messages received by potential buyers is the proper measure of advertising intensity suggested by economic theory, and this is the measure employed in this study.

Conclusions

In this chapter we have considered the problems of measuring profitability and advertising. Fisher and McGowan (1983) and Fisher (1986) have shown that the accounting rate of return on assets (or equity) and the rate of return on sales do not provide information about a firm's level of monopoly power. Therefore an alternative measure is required to test the hypothesis that advertising increases monopoly power. Martin (1985) has shown that market power does have observable consequences. When a firm has market power, the firm's market share has a significant effect on the accounting rate of return (measured as the return on sales or on assets). Therefore, if advertising increases monopoly power, it should cause increases in the accounting rate of return, and this condition should be satisfied if advertising creates barriers to entry.

Previous empirical work has often employed the advertising–sales ratio as a measure of advertising intensity. While this measure can be derived from the profit-maximizing behavior of the firm, it is not an appropriate measure of advertising intensity. No theory of consumer demand implies that buyers respond to the level of advertising expenditures or to the advertising–sales ratio. The theories that have modeled consumer response to advertising indicate that consumers must observe an advertising message before they can respond to it, and this is true whether advertising changes preferences or provides information. Advertising cannot change consumer tastes if it is not observed; therefore the appropriate measure of advertising intensity is the number of advertising messages received by potential customers. This measure has been employed in a few studies (Schmalensee [1972], Ehrlich and Fisher [1982]) and it is the measure of advertising intensity used in this research.

Having resolved important measurement issues that are crucial to the empirical tests, the next task is to discuss the causal tests themselves. These tests are presented along with the test results in the next chapter.

Notes

1. See Peles (1971), Bloch (1974), and Ayanian (1975, 1983).
2. See the exchange between Bloch (1980) and Comanor and Wilson (1979, 1980).

3. See Judge et al. (1980), p. 513.

4. Martin (1985) derives the comparative static properties of equation 4.7. Intuitively, if the firm wants to increase output to take advantage of economies of scale, then it must reduce the price of the product. Martin shows that the price will fall by more than the decline in marginal costs, and this will cause the return on sales to fall.

5. Albion and Farris (1981), p. 9.

6. See the models developed by Butters (1977), Ehrlich and Fisher (1982), Schmalensee (1983), and Fudenberg and Tirole (1984).

5
Causal Tests and Results

I n the previous chapters we established that the theories of advertising have different implications regarding the effects of advertising on competition. The causal tests used to test these theories of advertising are described and discussed in this chapter. Granger's (1969) concept of causality is presented and analyzed in the section "Testing for Causation." The specific causal implications of the two competing hypotheses of advertising (advertising as an entry barrier versus advertising as information) are discussed in "Testing the Advertising Hypotheses." Some important aspects of the causal tests themselves and their interpretation are then presented in the section, "Interpreting the Causal Tests." In "Data and Transformations" the specific data and transformations employed in this study are discussed, and the results of the tests and concluding remarks follow in the sections, "Empirical Results" and "Conclusions."

Testing for Causation

The causal relation between advertising and market power remains a key issue in the advertising debate. In the preceding chapter we found that when advertising increases market power, it should cause increases in the accounting rate of return. Since economists cannot perform controlled experiments, determining cause and effect requires some care. Granger (1969) developed an operational definition of causality which provides economists with a statistical view of causation. This is not the only view of cause and effect, and it does not correspond to the philosophical definition of causality (see Zellner [1979]). These points are important because they do influence how we interpret the Granger tests and the results that follow.

Granger defined causation in terms of prediction. Consider a bivariate time series (X_t, Y_t) that is linear, covariance stationary, and nondeterministic.[1] Granger argued that if Y_t helps to predict X_t, then Y_t is said to cause X_t. This definition emphasizes the predictability of a series and the role played by the flow of time. Since the future cannot cause the past, Granger argues that a time series, X_t, is caused by another series, Y_t, when past values of Y_t help to predict current values of X_t after accounting for past values of X_t.

Granger's definition of causality arises from statistical considerations. Some economists, such as Zellner (1979) and Harvey (1981), have argued that this approach is too limited and that a more general definition of causation is needed for economic research. Despite the limitations of this approach, the two competing theories of advertising can be tested using Granger's methodology because both imply a specific relationship between current advertising and future profits. While the Granger definition may be too limited as a general test of causation in economics, it can be used to determine if certain timing patterns implied by economic theory exist in the data. With this interpretation in mind, we will consider Granger's approach in more detail.

Suppose a variable, X_t, is regressed against its own past values and against past values of another variable, Y_t. According to Granger's definition, Y_t causes X_t if some of the past values of Y_t help predict X_t (if past Y are statistically significant in the regression). Since the future cannot cause the past, Granger's test focuses on the past predicting the future. Thus if u_t is a white noise process (that is, it has zero mean and is not correlated with itself over time) in the regression below,

$$X_t = a + \sum_{i=1}^{n} b_i X_{t-i} + \sum_{i=1}^{m} c_i Y_{t-i} + u_t, \qquad (5.1)$$

then Y does not "Granger-cause" X if and only if the c_i coefficients are jointly insignificantly different from zero. If any of the c_i coefficients are statistically significant (or if they are jointly significant), then Y is said to Granger-cause X. If Y Granger-causes X yet X does not Granger-cause Y, we have unidirectional causality from Y to X. If X Granger-causes Y as well, then feedback exists between the two stochastic processes.

Sims (1972) proposed an alternative formulation of the test outlined above. If the bivariate time series (X_t, Y_t) has an autoregressive representation (that is, if we can express $[X_t, Y_t]$ using only past values of the two series), then Y can be expressed as a distributed lag function of current, past, and future values of X alone. Using Sims's test, Y does not Granger-cause X if and only if in the two-sided regression of Y on X below, the c_i coefficients on *future* X values are not jointly significantly different from zero.

$$Y_t = a + \sum_{i=0}^{n} b_i X_{t-i} + \sum_{i=1}^{m} c_i X_{t+i} + u_t, \qquad (5.2)$$

Equation 5.2 is Sims's version of the Granger test for causality. In Sims's test,

Y causes X if current values of Y have a significant effect on future values of X. A conventional F-test or Chi-Square test can be used to test the hypothesis that the c_i coefficients are jointly significantly different from zero. It is crucial in both tests that the error terms are white noise processes (serially uncorrelated random variables) and that they are uncorrelated with the variables on the right-hand side of equations 5.1 and 5.2. When the bivariate time series has an autoregressive representation, Sims's test is equivalent to Granger's test.

Several important points must be made before proceeding to the empirical tests in this chapter. First, the causal tests require that the (X_t, Y_t) process is a covariance stationary process. Few economic time series are stationary. As a result, economists generally transform (filter) the series to make them stationary. Usually a series can be made stationary by differencing. As Zellner (1979) and Harvey (1981) emphasize, the nature of the filter applied to the data can affect the results of the causal tests, so care is required when transforming the data. Second, the length of the leads and lags (n and m) of the series involved is crucial in both tests. If values for n and m are set too low, the series may be truncated prematurely and this biases the results. Third, if the error terms in the estimating equations are not white noise processes, the results may be affected. Finally, a reminder that the definition of causality employed in these tests is based upon statistical requirements, not economic or philosophical requirements.

Testing the Advertising Hypotheses

The hypothesis that advertising creates entry barriers asserts that the firm's elasticity of demand is reduced by advertising expenditures. If this theory is correct, then increasing advertising outlays in one period should Granger-cause a reduction in (the absolute value of) the firm's elasticity of demand in future periods or increase its market share. This is a testable implication of the barrier-to-entry hypothesis: advertising should have a significantly negative effect on future (absolute) values of the elasticity of demand and a positive effect on market share. As we have shown in chapter 4, the accounting rate of return increases when the market power of the firm increases. Therefore if advertising outlays create a barrier to entry, they should increase the firm's market power and *raise* the accounting rate of return. Current advertising expenditures should increase future values of the return on sales if advertising increases market power. This is the condition advertising expenditures should satisfy if advertising creates entry barriers. Several notable features of the causal tests will be discussed in the next section regarding omitted variables problems and spurious correlation.

The information theory of advertising presented by Telser (1978), Nelson (1974), and Ehrlich and Fisher (1982) claims that advertising increases competition. If advertising has any effects on the firm's elasticity of demand, it should cause an increase in the absolute value of the elasticity over time. In the model developed by Ehrlich and Fisher, advertising, price, and profitability are all determined simultaneously. This should lead to a strong correlation between current advertising expenditures and current values of the accounting rate of return. However, the information theory does not necessarily predict that future values of the elasticity of demand will be affected by current advertising. To the extent that current expenditures on advertising do increase future competition, they should increase (the absolute value of) the elasticity of demand and *reduce* future values of the accounting rate of return.

The theories developed by Horowitz (1970) and Sherman and Tollison (1971, 1972) imply that the advertising–profits correlation is due to risk-related variables. Advertising and profits are contemporaneously correlated because variables measuring risk are omitted from the regressions. This approach implies that current advertising and current profits will be correlated. However, current advertising should not affect future profits.

The causal tests employed in this chapter test these predictions. How are future values of the return on sales affected by current advertising expenditures? If current advertising has positive effects on the future values of the return on sales, then the barrier-to-entry hypothesis is supported, subject to the qualifications presented below. If there is a strong correlation between current advertising outlays and the return on sales and negative or zero effects on future values, then the information and risk hypotheses are supported.

The estimating equation used to test for the causal effects of advertising is:

$$A_t = a + \sum_{i=0}^{n} b_i ROS_{t-i} + \sum_{i=1}^{m} c_i ROS_{t+i} + u_t, \tag{5.3}$$

where A_t is real advertising messages at time t and ROS_t is the rate of return on sales at time t. If advertising today increases monopoly power, it will increase the rate of return on sales in the future, and the c_i coefficients will be significant and positive. This result would support the view that advertising creates a barrier to entry which allows firms to raise their returns over time. On the other hand, if the c_i coefficients are negative or insignificantly different from zero, then current advertising will cause the return on sales to fall in the future (or it will have no effects on future returns). This result would be consistent with the view that advertising provides information to consumers or that risk-related variables affect advertising outlays.

Since the causal tests examine the effects of advertising on the rate of return over time, the dynamic influence of these outlays are observed in this study. This is an improvement over earlier work, most of which focused on the relationship between advertising and accounting profits at a single point in time. These cross-section tests cannot indicate whether advertising increases market power over time. Spurious factors may lead to an observed relationship between advertising and profits in the short run that has nothing to do with advertising causing higher profits. These problems (and several others, as we will see in the next section) are avoided with time series data.

Interpreting the Causal Tests

Several points concerning the causal tests must be clarified before proceeding. First, as indicated in the previous chapter, the return on sales reflects several factors in addition to market power, such as economies of scale and average costs. Therefore it is possible that the return on sales is an imperfect measure of market power and this could bias the test results when other variables are omitted from the regression. Although there is a measurement error, it is not likely to bias the causal tests.

Consider the Sherman–Tollison (1972) argument that the return on sales reflects technological factors in production (cost-fixity). They argued that firms would advertise more when fixed costs were high, and high fixed costs are likely to be associated with a high return on sales. Thus cost-fixity will cause a positive correlation between current levels of advertising and the current return on sales which would be observed in cross-section studies. However, it is unlikely that current advertising will affect *future* values of the return on sales even if the cost-fixity hypothesis is correct because current advertising will not change future levels of cost-fixity. Therefore the test of the barrier-to-entry hypothesis that current advertising affects future values of the return on sales is not affected by the Sherman–Tollison argument, and there is no bias from omitting measures of cost fixity.

Similarly, from equation 4.11 in chapter 4, the return on sales is also affected by economies of scale. An increase in advertising could cause an increase in output which might increase the importance of scale economies, MC/AC. According to equation 4.11, this would reduce the return on sales even if advertising increases the firm's market power. In this case it might appear that the tests will fail to measure the effects of advertising on market power because a relevant variable, economies of scale, has been omitted. However, economies of scale reduce the return on sales in equation 4.11 (and in Martin's [1985] model) because of the assumption that the firm must reduce its price to increase output. But when firms advertise, they can increase their output without reducing prices. Therefore even if advertising increases output and causes economies of scale to become more important, the return on sales will not necessarily fall. As long as the return on sales does not fall because of advertising-induced economies of scale, the causal tests will measure the effects of advertising as a barrier to entry.

In testing for the effects of advertising, the causal tests are likely to detect the effects of advertising on market power. Omitting an economies-of-scale variable will not bias the tests as much as equation 4.11 might suggest, particularly since the sample period extends over twenty-five years. It is unlikely that advertising can cause an increase in output and increase the importance of economies of scale in production over such a long period while the accounting return falls. The tests would be biased only if future economies of scale varied systematically with current advertising, so that future returns on sales would fall—and this is a remote possibility.

Several other variables included in Martin's (1985) model but omitted from the empirical work that follows are even less likely to bias the causal tests. Martin found that the return on sales could be affected by the capital–sales ratio, the dilution of ownership when new shares are issued, and the ratio of bond interest payments made by the firm to sales. Although these variables affect the return on sales in addition to the effect of advertising, it is unlikely that current advertising will cause these variables to change in the future. For example, it is unlikely that current advertising affects future values of the capital–sales ratio (although it is possible that current values of the capital sales ratio will influence the future level of advertising via the cost-fixity effect). Current advertising should also have no effects on future measures of ownership dilution or bond interest payments.

When variables are omitted from the regression, the estimated coefficients will be biased if the omitted variables are correlated with advertising outlays. Such a correlation was likely in many of the previous tests of the advertising–profits relation because they employed cross-section data. In cross-section studies, cost-fixity variables and capital–sales ratios are likely to be correlated with advertising expenditures. Because time series data and time series tests are used in this study, many of the previous omitted variables arguments are not relevant because the correlation these arguments stressed in cross-section studies is not likely to occur over time.

The same line of reasoning can also be applied to Fisher's (1986) criticisms of the return on sales. He argued that the measurement error from using the return on sales as a proxy for the Lerner index of monopoly power would be correlated with many variables used to explain profitability, such as the depreciation methods used by the firm, capital intensity, and risk. However, advertising should not cause changes in these variables over time, and therefore omitting these variables should not bias the tests. Therefore we could interpret the return on sales as a measure of the Lerner index of monopoly power without altering the interpretation of the test results. Fisher is correct in arguing that the return on sales is a poor proxy for the Lerner index, but the measurement bias he emphasizes is not likely to appear in these time series tests. The level of advertising today should not be correlated with the measurement error in future values of the Lerner index.

Finally, it is important to note that many other variables that could affect the return on sales are not included in this study. This normally causes omitted variables bias in the regression estimates. Although some of the omitted variables arguments could be dismissed, isn't it possible that other theories suggest additional sources of bias that we cannot ignore? If this is true, then the results obtained from this study may suffer from bias.

Fortunately this is not a problem in those cases where there is no evidence of a causal relation. If advertising does not cause monopoly power in the tests that follow, it is not likely that advertising will cause monopoly power in tests where more variables are included. This is because the results from bivariate causal tests imply restrictions on higher order (multivariate) systems. Specifically, Skoog (1976) has shown that if y_t, x_t, and z_t are weakly stationary stochastic processes, if x_t does not cause y_t bivariately, then in general, x_t does not cause y_t trivariately. This occurs because of the nature of the causal tests. If a third variable, z_t, were truly causing y_t, then we might find x_t spuriously causing y_t if z_t were omitted from the regression. However, it is very unlikely that *no* causal relation will be found if relevant variables have been omitted from our regressions.

Therefore, if we find that advertising does *not* cause changes in the rate of return in our regressions, Skoog's results imply that we are unlikely to find that advertising causes profits when more variables are added to the regressions. However, the reverse argument does not hold; if we discover that advertising "causes" changes in the return on sales in the work that follows, that result may not hold when more regressors are added. In this respect, the barrier-to-entry hypothesis will not receive strong support when there is evidence that advertising positively affects the return on sales. When a causal relation is discovered between advertising and the return on sales, the results could be due to spurious correlation, and in this case, if more explanatory variables were added to the regression, the causal results might change. However, the tests are much stronger in those cases where there is no evidence of a causal effect; the conclusions are not likely to change if more variables are included in the study.

Data and Transformations

One of the important contributions of this study is a new data source that has not been used in previous work. Each year since 1955, *Advertising Age* has collected and published annual advertising figures for the top one hundred firms in total advertising expenditures. The published data include total advertising outlays in "unmeasured media" (which measure sales and promotional efforts in addition to media advertising), and outlays in specific "measured media." *Advertising Age* mailed their estimates of unmeasured advertising outlays to the firms for confirmation and correction, but many firms did not respond. As a result, the unmeasured media figures are very unreliable and vary considerably from year to year (as discussed in chapter 4). In some years the firms added other selling expenses to their media advertising figures; in other years they did not.

The measured media data were gathered directly from media sources and are therefore more accurate. The media surveyed were: network television, spot television, network and spot radio, magazines, newspapers, and outdoor advertising. *Advertising Age* also published figures on the amount spent on each of the seven media by firm. This advertising data was matched with observations on sales and net income from *Moody's Industrial Manual*.

In chapter 4 it was argued that a price index for advertising was needed to measure advertising intensity. Several researchers (notably Schmalensee [1972] and Ehrlich and Fisher [1982]) developed price indices for the cost of advertising. These indices were then used to deflate the total advertising outlays for each industry to obtain real advertising expenditures. Generally, the fraction of industry expenditures on each of the media was used to determine the weights in the price index. So if the tobacco industry spent 20 percent of its advertising budget on network television, the cost of network television advertising would receive a weight of 20 percent in the advertising price index for the tobacco industry in that year. The problem here is that individual firms in an industry may purchase very different amounts of network advertising as a percentage of the advertising budget. For example, in 1983 R.J. Reynolds spent 29 percent of its advertising budget on network television while American Brands spent only 14.5 percent of its budget in this way. Firms with the same total advertising budget may spend that budget very differently among the seven media included in the sample. Clearly average industry costs for advertising are not accurate when there are wide variations in media outlays between the firms in an industry.

Since *Advertising Age* provides data on the percentage of the advertising budget spent on each of the seven media by each firm, a price index for advertising was developed for *each company* in the sample.[2] Therefore a better measure of the number of advertising messages delivered by each firm is obtained here compared with earlier research. Firm-specific weights for the advertising price index should also improve the accuracy of the results obtained in this study compared with previous work.

The firm-specific data employed in this study are important for another reason. Henning and Mann (1976) attempted to test the causal relation between advertising and profits using an indirect test with industrywide data. It is unclear why this data is useful in testing for causality. First, advertising decisions are made at the level of the firm, not the industry.[3] Perhaps more important, industry data may *obscure* the causal relation. At the firm level, an increase in advertising by firm A may increase its profits and monopoly power, but reduce the profits of firm B. If we use industry data, the increase in industry advertising may not appear to raise industry profits (since the decline in firm B's profits may offset the rise in firm A's profits), yet advertising could still cause profit changes at the firm level. This criticism also applies to the recent causal study by Ashley, Granger and Schmalensee (1980) which used national advertising and consumption data. They found that national expenditures on advertising did not cause increases in total consumption spending in the United States. But this tells us nothing about the effects advertising has on competition between firms. If we want to know whether advertising by firms can increase their monopoly power, we must use firm-specific data.

To test the advertising–monopoly power relationship, all variables were transformed into growth rates by calculating $(X_t - X_{t-1})/X_t$ for real advertising outlays and the return on sales. In most cases, this transformation will make the time series for these variables stationary, although the variables were also regressed against a constant, and a time trend, and time squared to eliminate all trend effects. Usually researchers "difference" the data after taking logs to obtain growth rates by calculating:

$$\log(X_t) - \log(X_{t-1})$$

This transformation could not be used in this study because for many companies net income was negative for one or more years. Since logarithms cannot be calculated for negative numbers, the more conventional transformation was not used. However, the difference in the logs is approximately equal to the rate of growth used in this study, and both transformation yield approximately the same results.

The return on sales was calculated as the ratio of net income to sales. Although this measure includes interest and depreciation costs that are often excluded from calculations of the ratio, including these costs should present few difficulties given the discussion of spurious correlation in the preceding section. Advertising expenditures should not cause future changes in depreciation and interest costs, so spurious correlation between advertising and this measure of the profit–sales ratio is unlikely. Therefore the results of this study should not be affected by this measure of the return on sales.

Finally, it should be noted that for several companies the fiscal year used to calculate profits is not the same as the calendar year used to determine the advertising figures. For example, the fiscal year for Pillsbury Mills ends in May, so yearly profits from May to April will overlap with the advertising data calculated from January to December. If Pillsbury advertised heavily in the last six months of 1965, the effects would not be recorded until the May 1966 profit statement. If advertising did not cause increases in future profits, but was contemporaneously correlated with profits, the difference in the reporting periods might cause the tests to falsely indicate a causal relation. In the example above, we might find a correlation between current advertising outlays and profits one period ahead. However, this timing pattern will only affect the relationship between profits and advertising one period into the future and should provide a bias in favor of the barrier-to-entry hypothesis. Despite this slight bias, the causal tests indicate little relationship between current advertising and future profits, as we will see in the next section.

Empirical Results

The appendix reports the causal test results for the twenty-seven firms whose advertising expenditures are available for the period from 1955 to 1983. Data for the rate of return on sales was calculated from 1948, so the sample period begins in 1956 even in those cases where the return on sales was lagged for six years. Since the advertising data is not available before 1954, Granger's original test and tests for reverse causation were not implemented. In both cases, lagging the advertising data would severely reduce the number of degrees of freedom for the regression. Since the debate has focused on the causal effects of advertising on market power, tests for reverse causation are not central to the argument.

Specification searches were conducted for all of the companies, with leads allowed up to four years into the future and lags extending back as far as six years into the past. The results were robust for most of the companies and were not sensitive to small changes in the number of leads or lags. In some cases the fourth lead was insignificant but had a substantial effect on the regression results, and in these situations, the fourth lead is reported in the tables. When reducing the number of lags had no effect on the regression estimates, insignificant lags beyond the third were omitted. Similarly, when the fourth lead did not affect the regression estimates, the tests were conducted with leads of three years. The equations were unstable for one company, Eastman Kodak, and several coefficients reversed sign when the equation for that company was corrected for serial correlation. Therefore lagged values of the dependent variable were added to the equation, as recommended by Geweke, Meese, and Dent (1983), and this stabilized the regression results.

When the regression equations were corrected for serial correlation, the unrestricted estimate of RHO was used in the restricted regression. For most of the companies, the Cochrane–Orcutt correction seemed to eliminate autocorrelation in the residuals, and time series analysis of the residuals confirmed this finding. The F-tests reported in the tables test the null hypothesis that all lead coefficients are jointly equal to zero. Since the power of the F-test declines as the number of the degrees of freedom falls, the number of leads and lags was kept as low as possible. Despite this effort, the F-tests were not particularly discriminating and these statistics alone are not a very reliable guide to the causal relation between advertising and market power.

The theories of advertising provide two different predictions about the causal relation between advertising and future returns on sales. Those companies with significantly positive lead coefficients provide support for the barrier-to-entry hypothesis (subject to the possibility of spurious correlation mentioned earlier). Those companies with nearly zero or negative lead coefficients provide support for the information or risk hypotheses (subject to possible omitted variables bias except in those cases where the leads are insignificant and small). The test results are summarized in table 5–1. Perhaps most surprising is the small number of firms for which current advertising and future values of the return on sales are positively correlated in any significant fashion.

As Sims (1972) recommends, it is important to consider the absolute size of the lead coefficients relative to the lag coefficients even when the lead coefficients are not significant. Large future coefficients may indicate feedback from the return on sales to advertising even when the coefficients are not statistically significant. Therefore several firms are included in the positive causal relation category because some of the positive lead coefficients were large, despite their large standard errors and the low F-statistics.

For more than two-thirds of the companies in the sample, advertising has insignificant or negative effects on future values of the return on sales. This contradicts the predictions of the barrier-to-entry theory. The effects of advertising on future returns are generally not durable even in those cases where a positive relation exists. For most of these companies the apparent effects of advertising outlays on future returns occur within the first few years. This is in sharp contrast to some earlier research where advertising was found to have effects over a substantial time period.[4] The results of this study are more consistent with the recent work of Ehrlich and Fisher (1982), where advertising was found to have short-term effects, if any.

In several cases where advertising did positively affect future values of the margin, the effects were negative in other lead periods. This might indicate that competitors matched the advertising expenditures of the firms in later periods or that the information hypothesis is correct and the margin ultimately falls when advertising increases. However, these explanations would imply that the lead coefficients are positive in the first few periods and are followed by negative coefficients in subsequent periods. Yet there is no consistent pattern in the signs of the lead coefficients for those companies in the positive lead category. Advertising had a consistently positive impact on

Table 5-1
Summary of the Causal Test Results: 1956-1980

Companies with Positive Lead Coefficients

1. Coca Cola	(no sign reversal)
2. Campbell Soup Co.	(no sign reversal)
3. Johnson and Johnson	(lead coefficients reversed sign)*
4. Kellogg Company	(lead coefficients reversed sign)*
5. PepsiCo Incorporated	(lead coefficients reversed sign)*
6. Reynolds Tobacco	(lead coefficients reversed sign)*
7. William Wrigley Jr. Co.	(no sign reversal)

Companies with Zero or Negative Lead Coefficients

1. American Home Products	
2. Bristol Meyers Co.	(negative)*
3. Chrysler Corp.	(zero)
4. Colgate Palmolive Co.	
5. Corn Products Company	(zero)
6. Ford Motor Co.	(zero)
7. Eastman Kodak Co.	(negative)*
8. General Electric Co. (zero)	
9. General Foods	(zero)
10. General Mills Co.	(zero)
11. General Motors Corp.	(zero)
12. Gillette Co.	(zero)
13. Liggett Group	
14. Phillip Morris Inc.	(zero)
15. Pillsbury Mills Co.	
16. Proctor and Gamble Co.	(negative)*
17. Quaker Oats	
18. RCA Corp.	(zero)
19. Sterling Drug Co.	
20. Warner Lambert Co.	(zero)

*An asterisk indicates that the lead coefficients were jointly significantly different from zero at the 95 percent confidence level. Those companies with lead coefficients that were relatively large but whose sign reversed in the three- to four-year lead period are so identified in the top portion of the table. This weakens the support for the barrier-to-entry hypothesis. Companies that had relatively small lead coefficients that were also insignificant are identified by (zero) beside their names.

future values of the margin for only three companies in the sample. For the remaining companies, if advertising increased the return on sales for some years in the future, it decreased future returns in other years.

Certainly the evidence does not offer much support for the view that advertising reduces competition. For most of the companies in the sample, advertising did not have significantly positive effects on the future return on sales, and these results indicate that advertising does not create a barrier to entry. For those companies with a positive relation, sign reversals occurred in several cases within the three- to four-year lead period, suggesting that competition is not uniformly reduced when companies increase their advertising outlays, and that the future effects of current advertising are often weak for the firms in this sample. The results of this study combined with Demsetz's (1982) arguments concerning barriers to entry indicate that public policy should proceed cautiously with any efforts to restrict advertising outlays.

Although many variables were omitted from these regressions, strong conclusions can be drawn for several of the firms. For those firms that have lead coefficients that are small and insignificantly different from zero, advertising does not appear to affect their market power. As Skoog (1976) has shown, if no causal relation is discovered at the bivariate level, it is unlikely that such a relation will be discovered at the multivariate level. Omitted variables bias is not a likely problem in these cases because it is probable that a causal relation between advertising and the margin would be discovered if relevant variables were omitted. Since no causal relation was discovered, omitted variables bias is not a problem. These companies are listed in table 5–1 with (zero) marked beside their names, indicating that the lead coefficients are relatively small in comparison with the other coefficients in the regression. In the other cases, although the lead coefficients may not be significant, they are large in absolute size relative to the lag coefficients, suggesting that some feedback may exist and that the results could change in a multivariate test (omitted variables bias could arise).

Although the test results do not support the barrier-to-entry hypothesis, this does not mean that advertising has no effects. If advertising affected market power within a very short time period (less than a year), the tests would fail to identify any effects. As Granger indicated, since the causal tests examine correlations between time periods, they will not identify any correlations that occur within the period. Therefore the barrier-to-entry hypothesis might be supported in tests that use a shorter sampling interval than the annual data employed in this study. If the annual time interval is too long, and if the barrier-to-entry approach is correct, then we should observe strong positive correlations between current advertising and current returns on sales. Listed below are those companies with significantly positive contemporaneous correlation between advertising and the return on sales:

1. Bristol Meyers Co.
2. Coca Cola
3. Corn Products Company
4. Ford Motor Co.
5. General Foods
6. Phillip Morris Inc.
7. Pillsbury Morris Inc.
8. William Wrigley Jr. Co.

Several companies which did not have positive lead coefficients do appear in the list, but the contemporaneous correlation could be due to omitted risk and information variables as well. By focusing on current period effects, the correlations reported in this list are subject to all the spurious effects that plagued the cross-section studies. Even in this case, the number of firms with significantly positive contemporaneous correlation is small.

The nature of the data used in this study may provide another explanation for the poor performance of the barrier-to-entry hypothesis. The advertising data gathered by *Advertising Age* measures domestic advertising expenditures in the measured media while the sales and profit data are worldwide totals for the companies. It is possible that advertising causes entry barriers and raises the domestic return on sales, but these effects are swamped by international effects. While plausible, this explanation requires a consistent, negative relationship between the international return on sales and the domestic return. Furthermore, international effects must be sufficiently large to overwhelm domestic performance, either because domestic operations are small relative to international operations, or because the size of international losses is so large. It seems unlikely that all the results of this study would be biased by such large and negative international effects, although they may be at work in specific cases.

Conclusions

After describing the causal tests, the two competing theories of advertising were tested in this chapter. The theory of entry barriers, which received strong support in cross-section studies, has been seriously criticized and challenged by recent theoretical and empirical work. Fisher and McGowan (1983) showed that accounting rates of return do not measure economic rates of return, rendering the statistical relation between advertising and "profits" much less clear.

As a result of these findings, time series tests were developed to test for the competitive effects of advertising using a new data source on advertising expenditures. Most of the previous empirical work has employed industry-wide advertising data, accounting profits, and the advertising–sales ratio in testing the effects of advertising. The discussion in chapters 3, 4, and 5 indicates that industrywide data are inappropriate and likely to lead to biased results in causal tests.

The results from the causal tests indicate that advertising does not seriously impair market competition for most of the companies in the sample. In those cases where advertising did positively affect future values of the return on sales, the lead coefficients often reversed sign and were not highly significant. Strong contemporaneous correlation exists between advertising and the return on sales for many companies, which supports the risk and information theories of advertising, and implies that advertising cannot be treated as an exogenous variable in empirical research. Schmalensee (1972), Strickland and Weiss (1976), Pagoulatos and Sorensen (1981) and Ehrlich and Fisher (1982) are among the few researchers to recognize that advertising outlays are not exogenous in their research.[5] Ordinary-least-squares regressions will yield biased coefficient estimates when advertising and profits are simultaneously related.

These results do not imply that there are *no* effects from advertising, even in those cases where the coefficients are zero. Advertising outlays could have a considerable impact within a year. If so, the causal tests would fail to pick up these effects, since the data are gathered on an annual basis. However, this also implies that the barrier-to-entry view is not well supported, since firms cannot easily build up large stocks of advertising goodwill over time if the effects of advertising last less than a year. Furthermore, if advertising creates a barrier to entry in less than a year, there should be a significant, positive correlation in the current period between advertising and the return on sales. There were few companies with significantly positive coefficients in the current period to support this interpretation, and these correlations also support the risk and information theories of advertising.

Although many relevant variables were omitted in these regressions, bias is less likely in these causal tests than in other cases. The test results could be weakened by the effects of international operations for some of these companies, but it is unlikely that international effects are sufficiently large and negative to bias all of the test results. Finally, many relevant variables have been omitted in this research which would normally bias the test results. However, in those cases where there is no evidence of a causal relation between advertising and the return on sales, Skoog (1976) has shown that omitted variables bias is unlikely. In this respect, the results are robust for those companies where advertising has no causal effects.

Notes

1. See Harvey (1981), pp. 300–307.
2. The index measures the cost of a standard message in each of the media per thousand viewers. The indices for media costs per thousand viewers were obtained from *Media Decisions* (fall 1984, August 1974, and August 1971) and were linked with the indices constructed by Schmalensee (1972). See Schmalensee (1972, Appendix A) for a detailed discussion of the index. These indices were then weighted by the firm's advertising outlays in each of the seven media, and the resulting cost index was used to deflate total advertising expenditures to obtain real expenditures in message units for the firm.
3. Comanor and Wilson (1979) argue that industry level data is appropriate because existing firms advertise to prevent entry. However, this assumes an implausibly high degree of collusion among the existing firms. Furthermore, it is often argued

that when firms do collude, they agree to set prices but then compete for market share by advertising and other forms of nonprice competition. Collusive industry behavior of this type argues against the use of industrywide advertising data.

4. For example, Clarke (1976) argued that annual data caused researchers to overestimate the duration of the effects of advertising. However, Clarke used nominal advertising expenditures in his study and did not stationarize his data. Finally, he used a constrained distribution lag procedure (Koyck and polynomial), which can bias the results, as Sims (1972) has argued. Ayanian (1983) found that advertising had durable effects, but his results are based upon the advertising-sales ratio for the industries he studied.

5. For example, Netters (1982) recently argued that advertising was exogenous because firms must set advertising levels before sales are determined. However, this does not establish that advertising expenditures are exogenous because firms may set advertising in anticipation of future sales and they may adjust current advertising levels with changes in current sales. If firms respond this way, then current advertising will be correlated with current sales and this is enough to bias least squares estimates.

6
Advertising and Public Policy

T hus far the analysis of the advertising debate has centered on the effects advertising may have on competition and efficiency. However, public and legislative interest has been more concerned recently with the influence advertising may have on the consumption of specific goods, such as cigarettes, alcoholic beverages, and children's products. Many consumer interest groups have recommended bans on all cigarette advertising and all broadcast advertising of alcoholic beverages.

In this chapter the effects of advertising and advertising restrictions are considered in terms of how they affect public welfare. An important issue debated in the economics literature is whether the volume of advertising supplied by markets is excessive relative to society's needs. Several models that examine this topic are reviewed in the section "Advertising and Social Welfare," and some of the insights from this research are then used to evaluate the effects of advertising bans in the following section, "The Welfare Effects of Advertising Restrictions." We consider several studies that estimate the effects of cigarette advertising bans in the section "The Effectiveness of Cigarette Advertising Restrictions." Although many researchers have attempted to measure the impact of cigarette advertising bans, the studies are frequently biased or misspecified. Therefore, in the following section, "Empirical Estimates of Cigarette Demand," new estimates of the demand for cigarettes in the United States are provided to determine whether the advertising ban reduced cigarette consumption. Conclusions follow in the last section.

Advertising and Social Welfare

It has been difficult for economists to theoretically analyze the effects of advertising on social welfare. In chapters 2 and 3 we considered two broad classes of models which disagreed on this important issue. The barrier-to-entry approach asserts that advertising reduces competition and social welfare when large firms are able to earn long-run economic profits by advertising. However, when advertising provides information, it improves efficiency and makes society better off, enabling consumers to make better decisions about their purchases. The difference between these two approaches centers on whether advertising changes tastes or provides information. Until recently, economic theory offered little guidance about welfare comparisons when tastes change. Economists must evaluate consumer's surplus, the area under the demand curve, in order to analyze social welfare. When advertising causes tastes to change, there will be two different values for consumer surplus, one for the pre-advertising demand curve and another for the post-advertising demand curve, and there is no reason to prefer one over the other for welfare calculations. Since advertising generally attempts to both inform and persuade consumers, it has been difficult to determine the effects of advertising on welfare.

Several recent models have been developed in an effort to avoid these problems and assess the welfare effects of advertising. Dixit and Norman (1978) presented a model in which advertising reduces the elasticity of the firm's demand curve by shifting demand to the right. Since the shift in demand could occur because advertising changes either tastes or information (or both), it appeared as though the model might provide clear conclusions about the effects of advertising. Dixit and Norman solved the problem of welfare comparisons when tastes change by evaluating the effects of advertising using both pre-advertising and post-advertising tastes as standards. When the two standards yield identical conclusions, there can be no question about the welfare effects of advertising. They then examined the profit-maximizing level of advertising that a firm would choose under monopoly, oligopoly, and monopolistic competition. From this analysis Dixit and Norman derived a strong result: firms often advertised too much in these markets, implying that society would be better off if advertising were reduced.

Dixit and Norman's conclusion that firms advertised excessively was controversial and generated several responses. Fisher and McGowan (1979) argued that if advertising changed tastes, as Dixit and Norman claimed, then welfare calculations should include the "good feelings" advertising creates, yet Dixit and Norman overlooked these effects. But Dixit and Norman countered that if advertising simply changed consumer's evaluations of products, it did not necessarily make them better off. Therefore there was no need to consider the good feelings created by advertising since advertising itself did not improve the consumer's welfare. Kotowitz and Mathewson (1979) and Shapiro (1980) argued that Dixit and Norman's results were not completely general. If advertising informs at least some consumers, then a monopolist might supply too little advertising. When at least some consumers are informed by advertising, those consumers are made better off and advertising will increase their welfare. Dixit and Norman (1980) agreed that when advertising provides information to new consumers, the conclusion that firms advertise excessively would not hold. However, when advertising changes tastes, their results were not affected. Once again the welfare effects of advertising seemed to depend on whether advertising changed tastes or provided information.

It appeared as though the tastes versus information issue would prevent further progress on the welfare effects of advertising, but recent work by Nichols (1985) has helped to identify cases where advertising will improve welfare. He extended the model of consumer demand developed by Stigler and Becker (1977), and argued that the market structure of the product markets was not important in determining the welfare effects of advertising. In Nichols's model, a monopolist might advertise too little and a perfectly competitive firm might advertise too much from society's viewpoint.

According to Stigler and Becker's model, consumers do not demand goods themselves, but the enjoyment that goods can produce when combined with the consumers' time, abilities, and the advertising supplied by the firm. Consumers use products as inputs to produce "commodities" that are the ultimate objects of satisfaction. For example, if an individual wants to enjoy painting, he or she will buy paint supplies in the market. But owning these supplies does not ultimately generate satisfaction—it is the commodity, "painting," that creates enjoyment. The consumer must use the paint supplies along with other inputs (time, skills) to enjoy the act of painting. Under this interpretation, some market goods will be more efficient than others in producing a desired commodity for the consumer. The "costs" of producing a commodity with market goods will depend upon the consumer's skills and knowledge. In our example, an oil painter may find watercolors a much more costly way to enjoy painting if she has little experience with watercolor techniques. Stigler and Becker contend that these costs of production are the "shadow" prices of the commodities, and that advertising can increase the productivity of the market goods used as inputs. They assert that advertising changes the costs of producing commodities with market goods even when it appears to change tastes in the product market.

Consider the tennis example presented by Nichols. He argues that consumers buy racquets and balls to play tennis, and that playing the game creates enjoyment. The commodity, "playing the game," is produced with tennis gear, the individual's skill, and time. If advertising tennis equipment improves a tennis player's enjoyment of the game, then advertising lowers the cost of playing the game for enjoyment. The insight here is that advertising reduces the costs of playing the game, and this causes a movement along the commodity demand curve even though the market demand curve for tennis equipment shifts.

Since advertising does not shift the *commodity* demand curve, Nichols asserts that we can measure consumer surplus as the area under the stable commodity demand curve. This analysis avoids the problem encountered in Dixit and Norman's model because it is not necessary to identify whether advertising changes tastes or provides information (or both). In both cases, advertising lowers the shadow price (cost) of the commodity consumers demand. This is similar to the analysis employed by Ehrlich and Fisher (1982). They asserted that advertising lowered the cost to the consumer of finding appropriate brands, although Nichols's treatment is more general since his model allows advertising to change tastes as well as inform consumers.

Using this framework, Nichols found that the market structure of the desired commodity determined whether advertising increased social welfare, not the structure of the markets for the purchased goods. If social status is the desired commodity, and consumers know it can be produced by many different products in the market, then the commodity market for social status is perfectly competitive and the level of advertising is optimal. Since consumers demand commodities, they can choose among many different market goods to produce them. This choice reduces the market power any single firm might have for its product because consumers can choose other products to achieve the same goals (to produce the same commodities).

Nichols also identifies a situation when firms will supply too much advertising. If advertising raises the market price of the product and also *increases* the shadow price of the commodity, then too much advertising has been supplied to the market. In this case, consumers purchase fewer units of the product as advertising increases, and society would be better off if firms advertised less. However, if advertising causes an increase in unit sales, then this is evidence that advertising is *undersupplied* and that firms should advertise more to increase social welfare.

Although Nichols' model is too simplified for policy recommendations, the analysis does clarify some important issues. A necessary condition for advertising to increase social welfare is that it increase unit sales. If unit sales decline, all else being equal, then advertising is oversupplied. In the section that follows we will consider the welfare effects of advertising restrictions. Nichols's necessary condition for socially optimal advertising has interesting implications regarding the effects of advertising bans.

The Welfare Effects of Advertising Restrictions

Welfare analysis of the effects of government policy is very difficult in even the best circumstances. But in those cases where a legal industry produces output which is believed to be harmful to consumers, the investigation becomes even more difficult. This is certainly the case with cigarettes and alcoholic beverages, and the intensity of the public debate concerning the advertising of these products reflects deep-rooted concerns on both sides of the issue. Since the products themselves cannot be completely banned, consumer interest groups and health organizations have sought to restrict advertising of these products.

Although the consumption of cigarettes and alcohol can be harmful, we will assume in the analysis that follows that consumers are sovereign and know what is best for them. While some might object to this assumption on paternalistic grounds, it is difficult to justify alternative assumptions in a world characterized by uncertainty and heterogeneous preferences (or heterogeneous "costs" in Stigler and Becker's framework). The crucial issue concerns the effects of advertising bans or restrictions on the markets for these goods.

Clarke and Else (1983) developed a model in which they examined the response of the market to advertising restrictions.[1] They assume that a monopolist produces a product and demand is determined by the quantity produced and the number of advertising messages sent to consumers. Although the solution to the model is rather involved, the conclusions reached by Clarke and Else are intuitively sensible. When advertising increases demand (as assumed in the model), public policies that reduce the level of advertising will reduce the amount consumed. The results obtained from this model would seem to support the conclusion that advertising bans will reduce consumption of the restricted products. However, this conclusion is not completely general,[2] and, as we will find later in this section, advertising bans may have perverse and unintended consequences.

Similar conclusions to those obtained by Clarke and Else can be illustrated using Ehrlich and Fisher's (1982) model of advertising discussed in chapter 3. In their model, price, advertising, and profitability are all determined simultaneously in the market by the forces of supply and demand. The consumers' demand for information gives rise to "indifference curves" along which the consumers' level of satisfaction is constant. These curves slope upward and to the right, indicating that consumers are willing to pay a higher price to obtain more information about products through advertising. Consumers are better off if they can obtain more advertising information at the same price, or if they can obtain the same advertising information at a lower price. This implies that consumers are better off on curves that lie to the right of $F_1 F_1$ in figure 6–1, while a curve such as $F_0 F_0$ represents a situation where consumers are relatively worse off. On the curve $F_0 F_0$, consumers must pay a higher price to receive the same level of advertising as on curve $F_1 F_1$, and this reduces their level of satisfaction.

Ehrlich and Fisher also show that suppliers are willing to provide advertising information to consumers if their profits are not reduced. Therefore a set of isoprofit curves can be derived along which the level of profits for the firm remains constant. In the diagram one such curve is $S_1 S_1$, which slopes

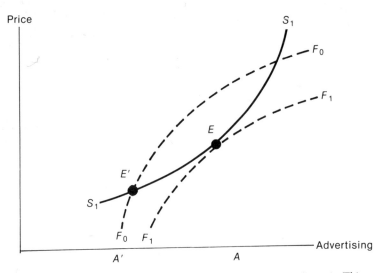

Note: Advertising restrictions reduce the level of advertising to A' from A. This moves the market to a new equilibrium at point E'. Consumers are worse off at the new equilibrium because they are paying a higher full price for the product. This places them on a lower "indifference" curve, F_0F_0. Consumers would prefer the previous equilibrium to E', but this is not possible when advertising levels are restricted.

Figure 6–1. Equilibrium Price and Advertising with Advertising Restrictions

upward to the right. This shows that if the firm increases its advertising, it must charge a higher price to keep the same level of profits. The market is in equilibrium when the firms' isoprofit curve is tangent to the consumers' indifference curve, as at point E in the diagram. If the industry is competitive, then the firms will be earning zero economic profits at this equilibrium, supplying the product and advertising at the lowest possible full price consumers are willing to pay. If the industry is not competitive, the firm(s) may be earning positive economic profits determined by the height of the isoprofit curve in equilibrium. In either case, equilibrium for the market normally occurs at the point where the two curves are tangent.

How will advertising restrictions affect the market equilibrium described in this model? If firms in the industry must supply fewer messages, the equilibrium at point E cannot be maintained. Suppose the firms are restricted to a level of advertising $A' < A$. This restriction will force the equilibrium to move to the left in the diagram. If the profits earned by the firms in this industry stay the same, the equilibrium will move along the isoprofit curve S_1S_1 to a new point, E'. If the firms in the industry compete to make consumers as well off as possible, then E' represents the best position consumers can attain. However, at this new equilibrium point consumers are worse off because they are now on the indifference curve F_0F_0 which represents a reduction in their well-being. This follows from the construction of the model because advertising provides information that consumers are willing to pay to obtain. If advertising restrictions are imposed on the industry, consumers are unable to obtain the information they need and this raises the full price of consuming the good. The reduction in advertising forces buyers to try more brands to satisfy their tastes, and this increases the cost of finding the right product.   if about insured

Ehrlich and Fisher assume that advertising provides information and that it is a valuable service. Therefore a reduction in advertising messages will make consumers worse off. Those who argue that advertising simply changes consumers' tastes would object to the assumption that advertising provides information, and might reject the welfare conclusions on those grounds. However, even when advertising changes consumers' tastes, it is not necessarily wasteful, as Nichols (1985) has shown (see below). Therefore it will be useful to consider the implications of an advertising ban with Ehrlich and Fisher's model.

Opponents of cigarette advertising (for example) object to the harmful effects cigarettes have on health. Therefore they recommend bans on cigarette advertising to reduce cigarette consumption and improve health. In the following section we will examine the statistical evidence that measures the effectiveness of advertising bans on cigarette consumption, but we can certainly assume that a complete ban on cigarette advertising would not end cigarette consumption. In fact, given the habitual nature of the product, we might expect little change in cigarette sales for several years. The important issues to consider are these: how will the advertising ban affect research and development in the cigarette industry, and how will the ban affect cigarette purchases?

It should be clear that if cigarette manufacturers are prevented from advertising, any expenditures on research and development will be less profitable. We would expect firms to reduce (if not stop) their efforts aimed at improving low-tar and nicotine brands. Cigarette firms have reduced incentives to develop "healthier" cigarettes if they cannot easily inform consumers about the relative virtues of the new product. This also means that those consumers who continue to smoke will be exposed to a greater health risk than they would be if cigarette companies continued to develop new, lower risk products and advertised them. Therefore, those who continue to smoke will have less opportunity to improve their health by consuming safer cigarettes. This is certainly possible if an advertising ban increases the costs for a firm to bring a safer product to market. The costs to society of the advertising ban will depend upon the number of smokers who continue to smoke, the probability that research and development will lead to safer cigarettes, and the degree of the improvement in smokers' health from the new product. Obviously a major health breakthrough in cigarettes may not be likely, but the advertising ban does impose an opportunity cost on society that its proponents overlook, and this cost may not be negligible. Certainly policy decisions would be improved if this cost were considered.

An advertising ban would also affect the purchases made by smokers. Those smokers who might want to switch to cigarettes with less tar and nicotine will have to devote more time and effort to accumulate the necessary information if cigarette advertising is banned. If the search required to find suitable brands is too costly, smokers would simply avoid switching to brands with lower health risks. Once again the advertising ban might prevent an improvement in smokers' health that would have occurred voluntarily. This opportunity cost may or may not be large, but it does require more care when assessing the effects of an advertising ban. In this light the conclusion obtained from the Ehrlich and Fisher model may not appear so counterintuitive. If advertising does provide some information to consumers about the relative risks from smoking different brands and gives firms the means to inform consumers about new products and to develop them, advertising bans will reduce social welfare, unless there are externalities created by cigarette advertising.

The model developed by Ehrlich and Fisher assumes that all advertising is informative. If we use the less restrictive model developed by Nichols (1985), the advertising ban will not unambiguously reduce welfare. For example, if the firms in the cigarette industry advertised excessively, so that advertising increased the shadow costs of smoking and reduced cigarette consumption, then reducing advertising expenditures would increase social welfare (as discussed in "The Welfare Effects of Advertising Restrictions" above). But if firms in the cigarette industry advertised excessively, then advertising levels would be so high that they would *reduce* cigarette consumption. So a ban on cigarette advertising could increase cigarette consumption in this case. According to Nichols's model, if a reduction in cigarette advertising would improve social welfare, it might also have the perverse effect of *increasing* cigarette consumption. This occurs because excessive advertising reduces the unit sales of the product and an advertising ban could decrease advertising enough to increase consumption.

On the other hand, if cigarette firms were not advertising excessively, then advertising restrictions would decrease social welfare in Nichols' model. In either case, whether advertising is over- or undersupplied by the cigarette industry, it would appear that proponents of the cigarette ban will not completely achieve their goals. If advertising is oversupplied, then welfare can be improved by an advertising ban, but the ban could actually increase cigarette consumption. If advertising is undersupplied, the ban will reduce cigarette consumption, but it will not improve consumer welfare. Overall, these theoretical results indicate that the advertising ban is not likely to improve social welfare—as would be expected since the ban does not allow the incremental adjustments necessary to achieve a welfare optimum. If social welfare is optimized by slight reductions in advertising, bans are likely to reduce advertising too much. Policymakers want to reduce consumption of certain products through advertising restrictions, yet they also want to improve social welfare. Our analysis shows that when advertising is supplied excessively, the ban may increase consumption even as it improves social welfare. If advertising is not oversupplied, then an advertising ban will reduce consumption but it will also reduce social welfare. Therefore advertising bans would not appear to be an optimal policy when these two goals (improving welfare and reducing consumption) are desired. These results would also apply to bans on advertising alcoholic beverages. In the next section we review several studies of the effectiveness of cigarette advertising bans and then new estimates are presented for the United States.

The Effectiveness of Cigarette Advertising Restrictions

Since the 1964 surgeon general's report on the health effects of cigarette smoking, the federal government has pursued policies to discourage cigarette smoking. In 1965, health warnings were required on cigarette packages, and in 1967, the Federal Communications Commission applied the Fairness Doctrine to cigarette advertising. This required broadcast stations that carried cigarette advertisements to offer free time for antismoking messages. When federal law banned all broadcast advertising of cigarettes in 1971, the requirement for equal time for antismoking messages ended and the number of these messages declined.

Many researchers have analyzed the economic effects of the cigarette advertising ban to determine if the ban reduced cigarette consumption. Several of these studies will be reviewed in this section, followed by new estimates of cigarette demand for the United States in the next section. Although numerous studies have estimated the demand for cigarettes, many of these studies are statistically biased.

In a well-known study Hamilton (1972) estimated the effectiveness of the 1971 ban on cigarette advertising. He argued that the 1964 surgeon general's report and the antismoking advertisements aired during the period of the Fairness Doctrine created "health scare effects" that were effective in reducing cigarette consumption. The 1971 ban on cigarette advertising significantly reduced the number of antismoking messages aired, but consumption of cigarettes actually increased after the ban. Many observers argued that the rise in cigarette consumption occurred because the ban was ineffective. Hamilton contended that the antismoking messages had a greater impact on demand than advertising by cigarette companies, so when the ban was imposed in 1971, cigarette consumption increased. He asserted that the antismoking messages were very effective in reducing cigarette consumption, and the decline in these messages in 1971 was responsible for the rise in consumption.

To test his hypothesis, Hamilton estimated a cigarette demand curve where the quantity of cigarettes consumed annually per capita was a function of per capita income per year, the relative price of cigarettes, annual per capita cigarette advertising, and dummy variables for the 1953 health report, the 1964 surgeon general's report, and the 1968 Fairness Doctrine period. Since the price and income variables were highly collinear, Hamilton used cross-section estimates of these coefficients and then estimated the remaining coefficients in the demand equation. He found that advertising had a very small, positive effect on demand but the coefficients for the 1968 antismoking dummy variables were negative and consistently larger than the advertising coefficients. This supported his hypothesis that the advertising ban was ineffective in reducing cigarette demand because it reduced the number of antismoking commercials.

Doron (1979) obtained similar results in his study. To avoid the multicollinearity problem, he combined the price and income variables together, but there is no justification for this transformation in economic theory, and it is not clear what is measured by the transformed variable. While his results agreed with those obtained by Hamilton, they are unreliable because the "demand" equation was estimated by ordinary least squares and was not identified. Ordinary-least-squares estimators are inconsistent when the independent variable is endogenous.[3] When price and quantity are determined simultaneously, regressions of quantity against price using ordinary least squares will yield biased estimates.

Similar problems with simultaneous equations bias and a failure to identify the demand equation plague three recent studies by Lewit, Coate, and Grossman (1981); Schneider, Klein, and Murphy (1981); and McLeod (1986). In their study of teenage smoking, Lewit, Coate, and Grossman estimated the demand curve for cigarette smoking by teenagers. The dependent variable in several specifications of their model was dichotomous—a value of one if the teenager smoked, zero otherwise. Lewit, Coate, and Grossman estimate the demand curve by ordinary least squares, a procedure that yields biased estimates when the dependent variable is dichotomous. Although they indicate that the results were similar when maximum likelihood procedures were employed, this does not eliminate the simultaneous equations bias nor does it serve to identify the demand curve. They mention in a footnote that the supply curve is assumed to be infinitely elastic in their model, and if this assumption were correct, then ordinary least squares would yield consistent estimates when the equation is identified. However, Lewit, Coate, and Grossman simply assume that supply is perfectly elastic, and studies of cigarette supply by Vernon, Rives, and Naylor (1969) and Bishop and Yoo (1985) indicate that this assumption is incorrect. In any event, the demand curve is not identified in the study, so little faith can be placed in their estimates.

Schneider, Klein, and Murphy (1981) claimed that previous estimates of the demand for cigarettes are misspecified. They contend that the 1953 health report and the 1964 surgeon general's report significantly affected cigarette consumption, but the effect of these reports has been overlooked because changes in cigarette technology have not been considered. As the public became aware of the dangers of cigarette smoking, cigarette companies introduced filter-tip and low-tar cigarettes. This change in cigarette technology reduced the amount of tobacco per cigarette and reduced the health risks of smoking. Therefore, Schneider, Klein, and Murphy argued, the cigarette demand curve should include variables that measure these changes in the quality of cigarettes. If not, researchers should estimate the demand for tobacco which will reflect the reduction in tobacco consumption. This is a valid argument, and it does help explain some of the anomalies in per capita cigarette consumption during the post-war period. They concluded that the advertising ban was not effective in reducing consumption, and that cigarette consumption had been declining steadily since the 1953 and 1964 health reports. However, the empirical results they obtained are unreliable since the demand curve is unidentified and was estimated by ordinary least squares.

A recent study by McLeod (986) analyzed the effects of the cigarette broadcast advertising ban in Australia, implemented in 1976. He found that advertising ban had immediate but short-term effects on per capita cigarette and tobacco consumption. Again, the demand curve was estimated by ordinary least squares (with a correction for serial correlation) and was not identified. Therefore these results are no more reliable than the others reviewed in this section.

One study where simultaneous equations bias and identification issues were considered was recently presented by Bishop and Yoo (1985). They estimated both the supply and demand curves for cigarettes in a simultaneous equations system. Their model is specified as:

$$Q_t^d = a_0 + a_1 P_r + a_3 DI + a_4 AD + a_5 D_{64} + e_1 \tag{6.1}$$

$$Q_t^s = b_0 + b_1 P_r + b_2 TX + b_3 FPI + b_4 D_{71} + e_2, \tag{6.2}$$

where Q_t is the log of the quantity of cigarettes consumed (all variables are logs except the dummy terms), P_r is the retail price index per cigarette, DI is an index of real disposable income, AD is an index of total advertising expenditures, D_{64} is a dummy variable for the 1964 surgeon general's report, and e_1 is an error term. For the supply curve, TX is the total federal and state tax per cigarette, FPI is a factor price index, D_{71} is a dummy variable for the

1971 advertising ban, and e_2 is an error term for supply. Bishop and Yoo argue that the primary effect of the advertising ban was to increase the costs of advertising because cigarette companies were forced to use less efficient media. They presented several sets of results estimating the supply and demand curves singly and as a system using two and three stage least squares. Bishop and Yoo obtained estimates of the elasticity of demand that ranged from -0.4 to -0.5, and they found that advertising expenditures had a significant, positive effect on demand, but the coefficient was very small. The dummy variable for the surgeon general's report was significantly negative and small as well. The elasticity of supply was positive ranging from 1 to 2.2, and the dummy variable for the advertising ban was negative and significant. Their results indicate that the cigarette market is a simultaneous system where quantity and price are both endogenous variables.

The study by Bishop and Yoo is the most careful of the time series tests reviewed in this section.[4] However, they did not estimate the per capita demand for cigarettes or the changes in cigarette technology emphasized by Schneider, Klein, and Murphy. Another potential problem concerns the treatment of the advertising variable. Bishop and Yoo used total advertising expenditures by the industry and did not deflate these figures to reflect the real advertising cost for each firm. Advertising expenditures were also treated as an exogenous variable in their study, yet the theories developed in chapters 2 and 3 suggest that advertising expenditure decisions are affected by sales. Therefore, it will be fruitful to estimate the demand curve for cigarettes in the United States considering these additional points.

Empirical Estimates of Cigarette Demand

The demand of cigarettes in the United States was estimated over the period from 1956 to 1983. Data for cigarette and tobacco consumption were obtained from *Agricultural Statistics of the United States* (1970, 1985). The price index for cigarettes was obtained from, the "Consumer Price Index for Selected Items and Groups Other Than Food" (from the *Handbook of Labor Statistics*). Total industry advertising expenditures were calculated by summing the advertising outlays for each of the cigarette companies. These expenditures were deflated by a cost index for advertising as described in chapter 4. The initial specification for the demand curve is:

$$Q_t^d = e_0 + e_1 P_r + e_2 DI + e_3 RAD + e_4 D_{64} + e_5 TPC + u_1, \quad (6.3)$$

where all variables are logs and Q_t is the number of cigarettes consumed, P_r is the relative price of cigarettes, DI is real disposable income, and RAD is the measure of real advertising expenditures by the industry. The term D_{64} is a dummy variable measuring the impact of the surgeon general's report, *TPC* measures pounds of tobacco per cigarette, and u_1 is an error term. Although a supply equation is not estimated here, several exogenous supply variables were used as instruments to identify the demand curve. These variables included the number of employees in the cigarette industry, total wages and salaries paid by the industry per cigarette (based on output in 1972), the number of cigarettes produced per employee, and D_{71} as a dummy variable for the 1971 advertising ban.

The results from estimating equation 6.3 by two-stage least squares are reported in table 6–1. The regression estimates were very unstable and changed considerably with slight modifications in the model or the instruments. When the equation was corrected for first-order serial correlation, the estimates for RHO were extremely high, indicating that the variables were not stationary. After differencing the data the equation was estimated again and the results appear in equation 2 in table 6–1. These estimates are much more stable, and the coefficients on price, the dummy variable, and the amount of tobacco per cigarette have the expected signs. The estimated price elasticity of demand is similar to estimates obtained in earlier studies by Sumner (1981) and Bishop and Yoo (1985). The dummy variable for the 1964 surgeon general's report is negative and statistically significant, confirming the health-scare effects cited in earlier work.

The coefficients for real disposable income and total real advertising are not significant, and they were not significant in reduced-form regressions. Advertising coefficients were frequently small in earlier studies, so the fact that the real advertising variable was not significant in this regression does not contradict earlier work. Perhaps more suprising is the result that real disposable income does not affect cigarette consumption in this equation, since most studies have found a positive income elasticity for cigarette demand. However, it does not seem intuitively plausible that income should have much effect on cigarette demand; it is hard to imagine people consuming more cigarettes because they earned a raise, especially given the health effects of the product. It may be possible that significant income effects were discovered in earlier studies because of statistical bias or because the data is not stationary in logarithmic form. The regression estimates of the equation in log form were sufficiently unstable that virtually any coefficient values could be generated. For several of these runs the real disposable income variable was positive and reasonable in size but the slightest changes in the instruments completely changed this result. Since the real income variable was not significant in the reduced-form regressions for the log of the equation, it seems unlikely that the variable was insignificant in equation (2) in the table simply because of differencing or the specification of the model.

Two additional regression equations are reported in table 6–1. In equation (3), the dummy variable for the 1971 advertising ban was added to the

Table 6–1
Estimates of Cigarette Demand: 1956–1983

1. $\log Q_t = 7.63 - .691\,P_r + .39\,DI - .047\,RAD - .012\,D_{64} + .29\,TPC$
   $\ (2.7)\quad\ (.37)\quad\ (.22)\quad\ (.05)\quad\ (.03)\quad\ (.5)$

   $R^2 = .96,\ D.W. = 2.11,\ RHO = .65.$

2. $\Delta \log Q_t = .031 - .334\,P_r + .09\,DI - .03\,RAD + .03\,D_{64} + .29\,TPC$
   $\ (.01)\quad\ (.158)\quad\ (.22)\quad\ (.02)\quad\ (.009)\quad\ (.18)$

   $R^2 = .54,\ D.W. = 1.76.$

3. $\Delta \log Q_t = .031 - .334\,P_r + .09\,DI - .03\,RAD - .03\,D_{64} + .29\,TPC + .003\,D_{71}$
   $\ (.01)\quad\ (.158)\quad\ (.22)\quad\ (.02)\quad\ (.009)\quad\ (.18)\quad\ (.01)$

   $R^2 = .55,\ D.W. = 1.79.$

4. $\Delta \log Q_t = 0.20 - .301\,P_r + .09\,DI - .02\,RAD - .04\,D_{64} + .37\,TPC$
   $\ (.01)\quad\ (.146)\quad\ (.21)\quad\ (.03)\quad\ (.010)\quad\ (.15)$

   $R^2 = .66,\ D.W. = 1.97,\ RHO = .226.$

Note: Standard errors are reported in parentheses. The quantity and real income variables in equation 4 are per capita. Instrumental variables in these regressions were real disposable income, D_{64}, D_{71}, the inflation rate, time, pounds of tobacco per cigarette, and total wage and salary costs per cigarette.

initial regression. The coefficient for this variable was not significant in the regression, indicating that the 1971 advertising ban was not effective in reducing cigarette consumption, which confirms the results obtained by other researchers. The cigarette demand equation was also estimated with per capita cigarette consumption as the dependent variable, and with per capita real disposable income as a regressor. These results are reported in equation (4) in table 6–1. The estimated price elasticity is similar in magnitude to the coefficient in equation (2), and the behavior of the other coefficients is much the same as in the previous regression: the dummy variable for the surgeon general's report is significantly negative and small, and the total real advertising and per capita real income variables are not significant. The only major difference is that the tobacco per cigarette variable becomes statistically significant. Since the basic results do not change when the model is expressed in per capita form, it appears that the study by Bishop and Yoo (1985) is not flawed for omitting this specification. However, it is not clear that the logarithmic specification is correct, the model may require differencing. Finally, these regressions were also computed with tobacco consumption as the dependent variable, and the results were qualitatively the same.

Conclusions

Despite considerable interest in the issue, it has been difficult to evaluate the welfare effects of advertising because welfare comparisons are ambiguous when tastes change. Dixit and Norman (1978) attempted to avoid this problem by using both pre- and post-advertising tastes as standards for comparison, but their results ultimately depended on whether advertising simply changes tastes or provides information. Progress was made on this issue recently when Nichols (1985) extended the model developed by Stigler and Becker (1977) and provided welfare conclusions about the optimality of advertising when both tastes and information change. This model was employed in this chapter to evaluate the welfare effects of advertising restrictions and an unusual result was obtained. In cases when advertising is oversupplied, restrictions could improve social welfare, but it is also possible that consumption of the advertised good will increase as a result of the ban. In cases where advertising is optimally supplied, advertising restrictions will reduce consumption, but they will also reduce social welfare.

Empirical studies of the effectiveness of the 1971 cigarette advertising ban were reviewed in "The Effectiveness of Cigarette Advertising Restrictions." Many of these studies used ordinary least squares to estimate the demand for cigarettes, and this technique yields biased estimates when prices and quantities are endogenous. Since both variables are normally endogenous in markets, the results of these studies are unreliable. The study by Bishop and Yoo (1985) used consistent estimation procedures to estimate both the supply and demand for cigarettes. They found that a simultaneous equation model best fits the data for the cigarette industry, that the demand curve was relatively inelastic, and that the 1964 surgeon general's report had a small but significant effect in reducing cigarette demand, while the 1971 advertising ban had no effect on cigarette demand.

The empirical estimates obtained in this study confirmed these results with the qualification that the double log model did not appear to be stationary. The dummy variable for the surgeon general's report was significantly negative in the cigarette demand equations but the dummy variable for the advertising ban provided no explanatory power. From the theoretical and empirical analysis in this chapter, it appears that advertising bans are not the best policy to improve social welfare and reduce consumption. Since the advertising variables were not significant in any of the regressions of cigarette demand, it also seems that advertising has little effect on cigarette consumption.

Notes

1. Clarke and Else wrote their comment in response to a model developed by Baye (1981). Baye analyzed the effects of a change in the price of advertising caused by an advertising ban, discussion of which is not appropriate here.

2. Although Clarke and Else argue that a decline in consumption is likely, their model does not guarantee this result. Baye (1983) offers an example where consumption might increase.

3. See Kmenta (1986) or any textbook in econometrics.

4. Sumner (1981) provides consistent estimates of the elasticity of demand from a cross-section sample of states, and Sullivan (1985) developed a more general model to determine the degree of competition in the industry. Unfortunately, these results do not provide information about the effects of the advertising ban.

Appendix
Causal Test Results

EQUATION 1

AMERICAN HOME PRODUCTS COMPANY

DEPENDENT VARIABLE IS   (A(t)-A(t-1))/A(t)

THE CURRENTLY ACTIVE OBSERVATION SET IS
(1956- 1979)

COCHRANE-ORCUTT ITERATIVE TECHNIQUE

FINAL VALUE OF RHO=   0.2572679
STANDARD ERROR OF RHO =   0.2014958

RIGHT-HAND VARIABLE	ESTIMATED COEFFICIENT	STANDARD ERROR	T-STATISTIC
CONST.	0.304691E-02	0.252971E-01	0.120445
DPROFS (4)	1.12188	0.952846	1.17740
DPROFS (3)	0.376702	0.902265	0.417507
DPROFS (2)	-0.459732	0.794515	-0.578632
DPROFS (1)	-0.200210	0.834844	-0.239817
DPROFS	0.408213	0.857924	0.475815
DPROFS (-1)	-0.466682E-02	0.539846	-0.864473E-02
DPROFS (-2)	0.354924	0.516285	0.687457
DPROFS (-3)	0.174341	0.514562	0.338815

R-SQUARED =   0.276622   NOBS=   23
R-BAR-SQUARED (ADJ FOR DF)= -0.136736
DURBIN-WATSON (0 GAPS) = 1.792999

F - STATISTIC = .362

The F statistic tests the null hypothesis that the future coefficients of DPROFS are jointly equal to zero. The variable DPROFS measures the growth rate in net income/sales. If RS is defined as net income divided by sales, then DPROFS = (RS(t)-RS(t-1))/RS(t).

EQUATION 2

BRISTOL MEYERS COMPANY

DEPENDENT VARIABLE IS   (A(t)-A(t-1))/A(t)

THE CURRENTLY ACTIVE OBSERVATION SET IS
(1956- 1979)

ORDINARY LEAST SQUARES

RIGHT-HAND VARIABLE	ESTIMATED COEFFICIENT	STANDARD ERROR	T-STATISTIC
CONST.	-0.106700E-01	0.148319E-01	-0.719395
DPROFS (4)	-0.788398	0.314580	-2.50619
DPROFS (3)	-0.247587E-02	0.307715	-0.804599E-02
DPROFS (2)	-0.644654	0.307460	-2.09671
DPROFS (1)	-0.538433	0.311378	-1.72919
DPROFS	0.724297	0.322255	2.24759
DPROFS (-1)	0.352436	0.309074	1.14030
DPROFS (-2)	0.350498E-01	0.294531	0.119002
DPROFS (-3)	0.150877	0.262728	0.574270
DPROFS (-4)	-0.189557	0.113596	-1.66869
DPROFS (-5)	-0.253882	0.103978	-2.44170

R-SQUARED =   0.677918   NOBS=   24
R-BAR-SQUARED (ADJ FOR DF)= 0.430162
DURBIN-WATSON (0 GAPS) = 2.180024

F - STATISTIC = 4.3

The F statistic tests the null hypothesis that the future coefficients of DPROFS are jointly equal to zero. The variable DPROFS measures the growth rate in net income/sales. If RS is defined as net income divided by sales, then DPROFS = (RS(t)-RS(t-1))/RS(t).

For regressions in which the Cochrane–Orcutt Procedure was used to correct for serial correlation in the error term, the unrestricted estimate of RHO was used in both the restricted and unrestricted regressions.

EQUATION 3

CAMPBELL SOUP COMPANY

DEPENDENT VARIABLE IS   (A(t)-A(t-1))/A(t)

THE CURRENTLY ACTIVE OBSERVATION SET IS
(1956- 1980)

COCHRANE-ORCUTT ITERATIVE TECHNIQUE

FINAL VALUE OF RHO=   0.1285566
STANDARD ERROR OF RHO =   0.2024304

RIGHT-HAND VARIABLE	ESTIMATED COEFFICIENT	STANDARD ERROR	T-STATISTIC
CONST.	-0.963114E-02	0.333037E-01	-0.289191
DPROFS (3)	0.323457	0.433700	0.745809
DPROFS (2)	0.759020	0.519838	1.46011
DPROFS (1)	0.630794	0.486722	1.29600
DPROFS	0.472037E-01	0.508698	0.927932E-01
DPROFS (-1)	-0.184948	0.605353	-0.305521
DPROFS (-2)	0.565011	0.597099	0.946261
DPROFS (-3)	0.305314	0.522538	0.584290
DPROFS (-4)	-0.435169	0.485636	-0.896080
DPROFS (-5)	0.654393	0.486207	1.34592
DPROFS (-6)	0.793033	0.389877	2.03406

R-SQUARED =   0.465162   NOBS=   24
R-BAR-SQUARED (ADJ FOR DF)= 0.053748
DURBIN-WATSON (0 GAPS) = 1.711942

F - STATISTIC = 1.06

The F statistic tests the null hypothesis that the future
coefficients of DPROFS are jointly equal to zero. The variable
DPROFS measures the growth rate in net income/sales. If RS is
defined   as   net   income divided by sales, then DPROFS =
(RS(t)-RS(t-1))/RS(t).

EQUATION 4

CHRYSLER CORPORATION

DEPENDENT VARIABLE IS   (A(t)-A(t-1))/A(t)

THE CURRENTLY ACTIVE OBSERVATION SET IS
(1956- 1980)

COCHRANE-ORCUTT ITERATIVE TECHNIQUE

FINAL VALUE OF RHO=   -0.3393237
STANDARD ERROR OF RHO =   0.1920134

RIGHT-HAND VARIABLE	ESTIMATED COEFFICIENT	STANDARD ERROR	T-STATISTIC
CONST.	0.438080E-02	0.251163E-01	0.174421
DPROFS (3)	-0.189766E-01	0.125409E-01	-1.51318
DPROFS (2)	-0.110412E-01	0.110270E-01	-1.00128
DPROFS (1)	-0.423666E-02	0.111420E-01	-0.380242
DPROFS	-0.203845E-01	0.115947E-01	-1.75808
DPROFS (-1)	0.959478E-02	0.116904E-01	0.820738
DPROFS (-2)	0.305718E-01	0.115095E-01	2.65622
DPROFS (-3)	0.587718E-03	0.113947E-01	0.515782E-01
DPROFS (-4)	-0.125745E-01	0.114948E-01	-1.09393

R-SQUARED =   0.518578   NOBS=   24
R-BAR-SQUARED (ADJ FOR DF)= 0.261820
DURBIN-WATSON (0 GAPS) = 1.760385

F - STATISTIC = 1.22

The F statistic tests the null hypothesis that the future
coefficients of DPROFS are jointly equal to zero. The variable
DPROFS measures the growth rate in net income/sales. If RS is
defined   as   net   income divided by sales, then DPROFS =
(RS(t)-RS(t-1))/RS(t).

EQUATION 5

COCA-COLA COMPANY

DEPENDENT VARIABLE IS   (A(t)-A(t-1))/A(t)

THE CURRENTLY ACTIVE· OBSERVATION SET IS
(1956- 1980)

COCHRANE-ORCUTT ITERATIVE TECHNIQUE

FINAL VALUE OF RHO=   0.3027709
STANDARD ERROR OF RHO =   0.1945432

RIGHT-HAND VARIABLE	ESTIMATED COEFFICIENT	STANDARD ERROR	T-STATISTIC
CONST.	0.117474E-01	0.299055E-01	0.392817
DPROFS (3)	0.393420	0.257155	1.52990
DPROFS (2)	0.534347	0.278271	1.92024
DPROFS (1)	0.350968	0.322547	1.08811
DPROFS	0.471249	0.336420	1.40077
DPROFS (-1)	-0.373162	0.333949	-1.11742
DPROFS (-2)	-0.365500	0.314264	-1.16303
DPROFS (-3)	0.149323E-01	0.282178	0.529183E-01
DPROFS (-4)	-1.42441	0.258648	-5.50712

R-SQUARED =   0.772285   NOBS=   24
R-BAR-SQUARED (ADJ FOR DF)= 0.650837
DURBIN-WATSON (0 GAPS) = 1.785291

F - STATISTIC = 1.5

The F statistic tests the null hypothesis that the future coefficients of DPROFS are jointly equal to zero. The variable DPROFS measures the growth rate in net income/sales. If RS is defined as net income divided by sales, then DPROFS = (RS(t)-RS(t-1))/RS(t).

EQUATION 6

COLGATE-PALMOLIVE COMPANY

DEPENDENT VARIABLE IS   (A(t)-A(t-1))/A(t)

THE CURRENTLY ACTIVE OBSERVATION SET IS
(1956- 1980)

COCHRANE-ORCUTT ITERATIVE TECHNIQUE

FINAL VALUE OF RHO=   0.2521188
STANDARD ERROR OF RHO =   0.1975302

RIGHT-HAND VARIABLE	ESTIMATED COEFFICIENT	STANDARD ERROR	T-STATISTIC
CONST.	-0.351030E-01	0.381448E-01	-0.920257
DPROFS (3)	-0.247195	0.278241	-0.888420
DPROFS (2)	-0.512561	0.328724	-1.55925
DPROFS (1)	-0.524377	0.328152	-1.59797
DPROFS	0.755611E-02	0.318362	0.237343E-01
DPROFS (-1)	-0.231346E-02	0.313732	-0.737399E-02
DPROFS (-2)	-0.361821	0.286816	-1.26151
DPROFS (-3)	-0.309889	0.245723	-1.26113
DPROFS (-4)	-0.229678	0.191972	-1.19641
DPROFS (-5)	-0.209290	0.118196	-1.77071

R-SQUARED =   0.478037   NOBS=   24
R-BAR-SQUARED (ADJ FOR DF)= 0.142489
DURBIN-WATSON (0 GAPS) = 1.785486

F - STATISTIC = .98

The F statistic tests the null hypothesis that the future coefficients of DPROFS are jointly equal to zero. The variable DPROFS measures the growth rate in net income/sales. If RS is defined as net income divided by sales, then DPROFS = (RS(t)-RS(t-1))/RS(t).

EQUATION 7

CORN PRODUCTS REFINING COMPANY

DEPENDENT VARIABLE IS   (A(t)-A(t-1))/A(t)

THE CURRENTLY ACTIVE OBSERVATION SET IS
(1956- 1980)

COCHRANE-ORCUTT ITERATIVE TECHNIQUE

FINAL VALUE OF RHO=   -0.1626358
STANDARD ERROR OF RHO =   0.2014065

RIGHT-HAND VARIABLE	ESTIMATED COEFFICIENT	STANDARD ERROR	T-STATISTIC
CONST.	-0.173608E-01	0.278738E-01	-0.622838
DPROFS (3)	0.249991	0.217229	1.15082
DPROFS (2)	0.401458	0.268860	1.49319
DPROFS (1)	0.379365E-01	0.275579	0.137661
DPROFS	0.341401	0.275186	1.24062
DPROFS (-1)	-0.221003	0.281180	-0.785984
DPROFS (-2)	-0.167796	0.291796	-0.575046
DPROFS (-3)	-0.196437	0.284293	-0.690966

R-SQUARED = 0.318094 NOBS=   24
R-BAR-SQUARED (ADJ FOR DF)= 0.019760
DURBIN-WATSON (0 GAPS) = 2.113700

F - STATISTIC = .75

The F statistic tests the null hypothesis that the future coefficients of DPROFS are jointly equal to zero. The variable DPROFS measures the growth rate in net income/sales. If RS is defined as net income divided by sales, then DPROFS = (RS(t)-RS(t-1))/RS(t).

EQUATION 8

EASTMAN KODAK

DEPENDENT VARIABLE IS   (A(t)-A(t-1))/A(t)

THE CURRENTLY ACTIVE OBSERVATION SET IS
(1959- 1979)

ORDINARY LEAST SQUARES

RIGHT-HAND VARIABLE	ESTIMATED COEFFICIENT	STANDARD ERROR	T-STATISTIC
CONST.	.0.300752E-02	0.160830E-01	0.187000
DPROFS (4)	-0.912876	0.233010	-3.91775
DPROFS (3)	0.243656	0.259549	0.938766
DPROFS (2)	-0.628315	0.243826	-2.57690
DPROFS (1)	0.237948E-01	0.256318	0.928332E-01
DPROFS	-0.226225	0.255789	-0.884421
DPROFS (-1)	0.225464E-01	0.246410	0.914997E-01
DPROFS (-2)	-0.641123	0.250309	-2.56133
DPROFS (-3)	0.803252	0.309376	2.59636
LMA2 (-1)	0.670384	0.234740	2.85585
LMA2 (-2)	-0.515744	0.175527	-2.93826

R-SQUARED = 0.816056 NOBS=   21
R-BAR-SQUARED (ADJ FOR DF)= 0.632111
DURBIN-WATSON (0 GAPS) = 1.754683

F - STATISTIC = 5.15

The F statistic tests the null hypothesis that the future coefficients of DPROFS are jointly equal to zero. The variable DPROFS measures the growth rate in net income/sales. If RS is defined as net income divided by sales, then DPROFS = (RS(t)-RS(t-1))/RS(t). The variable LMA2 is the rate of growth in real advertising expenditures.

EQUATION 9

FORD MOTOR COMPANY

DEPENDENT VARIABLE IS   (A(t)-A(t-1))/A(t)

THE CURRENTLY ACTIVE OBSERVATION SET IS
(1956- 1980)

COCHRANE-ORCUTT ITERATIVE TECHNIQUE

FINAL VALUE OF RHO=   -0.2932875
STANDARD ERROR OF RHO =   0.1951476

RIGHT-HAND VARIABLE	ESTIMATED COEFFICIENT	STANDARD ERROR	T-STATISTIC
CONST.	-0.203225E-02	0.203933E-01	-0.996524E-01
DPROFS (3)	-0.399310E-01	0.245740E-01	-1.62492
DPROFS (2)	-0.667041E-02	0.242359E-01	-0.275229
DPROFS (1)	-0.436367E-01	0.254984E-01	-1.71135
DPROFS	0.634344E-01	0.251661E-01	2.52063
DPROFS (-1)	-0.859687E-02	0.259198E-01	-0.331671
DPROFS (-2)	0.146235E-01	0.258707E-01	0.565254
DPROFS (-3)	0.467391E-01	0.259245E-01	1.80289
DPROFS (-4)	0.200179E-02	0.252450E-01	0.792946E-01
DPROFS (-5)	-0.489235E-01	0.253899E-01	-1.92689

R-SQUARED =   0.663640   NOBS=   24
R-BAR-SQUARED (ADJ FOR DF)= 0.447409
DURBIN-WATSON (0 GAPS) = 1.903759

F - STATISTIC = 1.22

The F statistic tests the null hypothesis that the future coefficients of DPROFS are jointly equal to zero. The variable DPROFS measures the growth rate in net income/sales. If RS is defined as net income divided by sales, then DPROFS = (RS(t)-RS(t-1))/RS(t).

EQUATION 10

GENERAL ELECTRIC COMPANY

DEPENDENT VARIABLE IS   (A(t)-A(t-1))/A(t)

THE CURRENTLY ACTIVE OBSERVATION SET IS
(1956- 1980)

COCHRANE-ORCUTT ITERATIVE TECHNIQUE

FINAL VALUE OF RHO=   -0.2867879
STANDARD ERROR OF RHO =   0.1955497

RIGHT-HAND VARIABLE	ESTIMATED COEFFICIENT	STANDARD ERROR	T-STATISTIC
CONST.	0.386377E-02	0.276043E-01	0.139970
DPROFS (3)	0.347249E-01	0.300888	0.115408
DPROFS (2)	-0.125967E-01	0.277603	-0.453767E-01
DPROFS (1)	-0.480735	0.297905	-1.61372
DPROFS	0.222009	0.289724	0.766277
DPROFS (-1)	0.729416	0.289578	2.51889
DPROFS (-2)	-0.289159E-01	0.265248	-0.109015
DPROFS (-3)	-0.164380	0.264102	-0.622412

R-SQUARED =   0.564300   NOBS=   24
R-BAR-SQUARED (ADJ FOR DF)= 0.373681
DURBIN-WATSON (0 GAPS) = 2.255003

F - STATISTIC = 1.16

The F statistic tests the null hypothesis that the future coefficients of DPROFS are jointly equal to zero. The variable DPROFS measures the growth rate in net income/sales. If RS is defined as net income divided by sales, then DPROFS = (RS(t)-RS(t-1))/RS(t).

EQUATION 11

GENERAL FOODS

DEPENDENT VARIABLE IS (A(t)-A(t-1)/A(t)

THE CURRENTLY ACTIVE OBSERVATION SET IS
(1956- 1980)

ORDINARY LEAST SQUARES

RIGHT-HAND VARIABLE	ESTIMATED COEFFICIENT	STANDARD ERROR	T-STATISTIC
CONST.	0.122276E-01	0.197792E-01	0.618207
DPROFS (3)	0.281008	0.203915	1.37806
DPROFS (2)	0.210711	0.211383	0.996824
DPROFS (1)	0.205512	0.215764	0.952487
DPROFS	0.577349	0.261350	2.20910
DPROFS (-1)	-0.155136E-01	0.222687	-0.696652E-01
DPROFS (-2)	-0.519202	0.226582	-2.29145
DPROFS (-3)	-0.243358	0.293238	-0.829900

R-SQUARED =   0.431561   NOBS=   25
R-BAR-SQUARED (ADJ FOR DF)= 0.197498
DURBIN-WATSON (0 GAPS) = 2.090042

F - STATISTIC = .86

The F statistic tests the null hypothesis that the future coefficients of DPROFS are jointly equal to zero. The variable DPROFS measures the growth rate in net income/sales. If RS is defined as net income divided by sales, then DPROFS = (RS(t)-RS(t-1))/RS(t).

EQUATION 12

GENERAL MILLS COMPANY

DEPENDENT VARIABLE IS   (A(t)-A(t-1))/(A(t)

THE CURRENTLY ACTIVE OBSERVATION SET IS
(1956- 1980)

COCHRANE-ORCUTT ITERATIVE TECHNIQUE

FINAL VALUE OF RHO=   -0.6454844
STANDARD ERROR OF RHO =   0.1559046

RIGHT-HAND VARIABLE	ESTIMATED COEFFICIENT	STANDARD ERROR	T-STATISTIC
CONST.	-0.210439E-02	0.147287E-01	-0.142876
DPROFS (3)	-0.121235E-03	0.148160E-01	-0.818274E-02
DPROFS (2)	0.173750E-03	0.162427E-01	0.106972E-01
DPROFS (1)	-0.638375E-02	0.170189E-01	-0.375098
DPROFS	-0.157588E-01	0.171634E-01	-0.918166
DPROFS (-1)	-0.174518E-02	0.171580E-01	-0.101713
DPROFS (-2)	0.624477E-02	0.170450E-01	0.366369
DPROFS (-3)	-0.492583E-02	0.162223E-01	-0.303646
DPROFS (-4)	-0.431563E-01	0.148926E-01	-2.89784

R-SQUARED =   0.500945   NOBS=   24
R-BAR-SQUARED (ADJ FOR DF)= 0.234783
DURBIN-WATSON (0 GAPS) = 2.128664

F - STATISTIC = .05

The F statistic tests the null hypothesis that the future coefficients of DPROFS are jointly equal to zero. The variable DPROFS measures the growth rate in net income/sales. If RS is defined as net income divided by sales, then DPROFS = (RS(t)-RS(t-1))/RS(t).

EQUATION 13

GENERAL MOTORS CORPORATION

DEPENDENT VARIABLE IS   (A(t)-A(t-1))/A(t)

THE CURRENTLY ACTIVE OBSERVATION SET IS
(1956- 1980)

COCHRANE-ORCUTT ITERATIVE TECHNIQUE

FINAL VALUE OF RHO=   -0.2197099
STANDARD ERROR OF RHO =   0.1991364

RIGHT-HAND VARIABLE	ESTIMATED COEFFICIENT	STANDARD ERROR	T-STATISTIC
CONST.	0.183368E-02	0.359145E-01	0.510567E-01
DPROFS (3)	-0.304365E-01	0.684264E-01	-0.444806
DPROFS (2)	0.361988E-01	0.599410E-01	0.603908
DPROFS (1)	-0.228001E-01	0.624013E-01	-0.365378
DPROFS	-0.207522E-01	0.726745E-01	-0.285550
DPROFS (-1)	0.586599E-01	0.112137	0.523110
DPROFS (-2)	-0.174683E-01	0.116870	-0.149467
DPROFS (-3)	-0.129383	0.150160	-0.861630

R-SQUARED =   0.123404   NOBS=   24
R-BAR-SQUARED (ADJ FOR DF)= -0.260106
DURBIN-WATSON (0 GAPS) = 2.054456

F - STATISTIC = .136

The F statistic tests the null hypothesis that the future coefficients of DPROFS are jointly equal to zero. The variable DPROFS measures the growth rate in net income/sales. If RS is defined as net income divided by sales, then DPROFS = (RS(t)-RS(t-1))/RS(t).

EQUATION 14

GILLETTE COMPANY

DEPENDENT VARIABLE IS   (A(t)-A(t-1))/(A(t)

THE CURRENTLY ACTIVE OBSERVATION SET IS
(1956- 1980)

ORDINARY LEAST SQUARES

RIGHT-HAND VARIABLE	ESTIMATED COEFFICIENT	STANDARD ERROR	T-STATISTIC
CONST.	-0.723024E-02	0.242280E-01	-0.298425
DPROFS (3)	-0.417679E-02	0.341395	-0.122345E-01
DPROFS (2)	-0.196121	0.337466	-0.581159
DPROFS (1)	-0.403280E-01	0.334425	-0.120589
DPROFS	-0.940456E-02	0.333549	-0.281954E-01
DPROFS (-1)	-0.690570E-01	0.317050	-0.217811
DPROFS (-2)	0.158842	0.288082	0.551375
DPROFS (-3)	0.485851	0.289601	1.67766
DPROFS (-4)	-0.122674	0.235488	-0.520934
DPROFS (-5)	0.310678	0.219476	1.41554

R-SQUARED =   0.270111   NOBS=   25
R-BAR-SQUARED (ADJ FOR DF)= -0.167822
DURBIN-WATSON (0 GAPS) = 1.999758

F - STATISTIC = .205

The F statistic tests the null hypothesis that the future coefficients of DPROFS are jointly equal to zero. The variable DPROFS measures the growth rate in net income/sales. If RS is defined as net income divided by sales, then DPROFS = (RS(t)-RS(t-1))/RS(t).

EQUATION 15

JOHNSON AND JOHNSON

DEPENDENT VARIABLE IS   (A(t)-A(t-1))/(A(t)

THE CURRENTLY ACTIVE OBSERVATION SET IS
(1956- 1979)

COCHRANE-ORCUTT ITERATIVE TECHNIQUE

FINAL VALUE OF RHO=   -0.2392163
STANDARD ERROR OF RHO =   0.2024605

RIGHT-HAND VARIABLE	ESTIMATED COEFFICIENT	STANDARD ERROR	T-STATISTIC
CONST.	0.546751E-02	0.230997E-01	0.236692
DPROFS (4)	-0.427278E-04	0.192253E-04	-2.22248
DPROFS (3)	-0.233178E-04	0.192118E-04	-1.21372
DPROFS (2)	0.507747E-04	0.193577E-04	2.62298
DPROFS (1)	-0.858759E-05	0.193377E-04	-0.444086
DPROFS	-0.208339E-04	0.193341E-04	-1.07757
DPROFS (-1)	-0.421085E-05	0.193460E-04	-0.217660
DPROFS (-2)	-0.223031E-04	0.191963E-04	-1.16184
DPROFS (-3)	0.197368E-04	0.191847E-04	1.02878

R-SQUARED = 0.583860   NOBS=   23
R-BAR-SQUARED (ADJ FOR DF)= 0.346065
DURBIN-WATSON (0 GAPS) = 1.833595

F - STATISTIC = 3.82

The F statistic tests the null hypothesis that the future coefficients of DPROFS are jointly equal to zero. The variable DPROFS measures the growth rate in net income/sales. If RS is defined as net income divided by sales, then DPROFS = (RS(t)-RS(t-1))/RS(t).

EQUATION 16

KELLOGG COMPANY

DEPENDENT VARIABLE IS   (A(t)-A(t-1))/A(t)

THE CURRENTLY ACTIVE OBSERVATION SET IS
(1956- 1980)

ORDINARY LEAST SQUARES

RIGHT-HAND VARIABLE	ESTIMATED COEFFICIENT	STANDARD ERROR	T-STATISTIC
CONST.	0.633816E-02	0.213237E-01	0.297235
DPROFS (3)	0.299988E-01	0.282410	0.106224
DPROFS (2)	-0.356345	0.295528	-1.20579
DPROFS (1)	0.680464	0.279728	2.43259
DPROFS	-0.242446	0.288313	-0.840911
DPROFS (-1)	0.270235	0.276618	0.976922
DPROFS (-2)	0.313047E-02	0.248026	0.126215E-01
DPROFS (-3)	-0.224304	0.250703	-0.894702
DPROFS (-4)	-0.357014E-01	0.259231	-0.137721
DPROFS (-5)	-0.363957	0.185581	-1.96117

R-SQUARED = 0.451290   NOBS=   25
R-BAR-SQUARED (ADJ FOR DF)= 0.122064
DURBIN-WATSON (0 GAPS) = 2.271080

F - STATISTIC = 2.39

The F statistic tests the null hypothesis that the future coefficients of DPROFS are jointly equal to zero. The variable DPROFS measures the growth rate in net income/sales. If RS is defined as net income divided by sales, then DPROFS = (RS(t)-RS(t-1))/RS(t).

EQUATION 17

LIGGETT AND MEYERS TOBACCO

DEPENDENT VARIABLE IS   (A(t)-A(t-1))/A(t)

THE CURRENTLY ACTIVE OBSERVATION SET IS
(1956- 1977)

COCHRANE-ORCUTT ITERATIVE TECHNIQUE

FINAL VALUE OF RHO=   -0.2282336
STANDARD ERROR OF RHO =   0.2124583

RIGHT-HAND VARIABLE	ESTIMATED COEFFICIENT	STANDARD ERROR	T-STATISTIC
CONST.	-0.102515E-01	0.333073E-01	-0.307785
DPROFS (4)	-0.268519E-01	0.171921E-01	-1.56187
DPROFS (3)	-0.337118E-01	0.171914E-01	-1.96097
DPROFS (2)	-0.372397E-01	0.153386E-01	-2.42784
DPROFS (1)	-0.969997E-02	0.165626E-01	-0.585655
DPROFS	-0.371859E-01	0.193611E-01	-1.92065
DPROFS (-1)	0.194724	0.305666	0.637048
DPROFS (-2)	-0.813062E-01	0.414651	-0.196084
DPROFS (-3)	-0.196781	0.370423	-0.531234

R-SQUARED =   0.515855   NOBS=   21
R-BAR-SQUARED (ADJ FOR DF)= 0.193092
DURBIN-WATSON (0 GAPS) = 2.056317

F - STATISTIC = 2.38

The F statistic tests the null hypothesis that the future coefficients of DPROFS are jointly equal to zero. The variable DPROFS measures the growth rate in net income/sales. If RS is defined as net income divided by sales, then DPROFS = (RS(t)-RS(t-1))/RS(t).

EQUATION 18

PEPSI COLA COMPANY

DEPENDENT VARIABLE IS   (A(t)-A(t-1))/A(t)

THE CURRENTLY ACTIVE OBSERVATION SET IS
(1956- 1980)

COCHRANE-ORCUTT ITERATIVE TECHNIQUE

FINAL VALUE OF RHO=   -0.3105639
STANDARD ERROR OF RHO =   0.1940307

RIGHT-HAND VARIABLE	ESTIMATED COEFFICIENT	STANDARD ERROR	T-STATISTIC
CONST.	-0.947161E-02	0.270724E-01	-0.349862
DPROFS (3)	-0.245695	0.317042	-0.774959
DPROFS (2)	0.362958E-01	0.366622	0.990007E-01
DPROFS (1)	0.926809	0.538993	1.71952
DPROFS	-0.668002	0.574783	-1.16218
DPROFS (-1)	0.394186	0.564456	0.698347
DPROFS (-2)	-0.759888E-01	0.474533	-0.160134
DPROFS (-3)	0.145975	0.440847	0.331124
DPROFS (-4)	-0.206305	0.464350	-0.444288
DPROFS (-5)	0.100118	0.428018	0.233910
DPROFS (-6)	-0.836227	0.399174	-2.09489

R-SQUARED =   0.458047   NOBS=   24
R-BAR-SQUARED (ADJ FOR DF)= 0.041160
DURBIN-WATSON (0 GAPS) = 2.187092

F - STATISTIC = 1.38

The F statistic tests the null hypothesis that the future coefficients of DPROFS are jointly equal to zero. The variable DPROFS measures the growth rate in net income/sales. If RS is defined as net income divided by sales, then DPROFS = (RS(t)-RS(t-1))/RS(t).

EQUATION 19

PHILLIP MORRIS INC.

DEPENDENT VARIABLE IS   (A(t)-A(t-1))/A(t)

THE CURRENTLY ACTIVE OBSERVATION SET IS
(1956- 1980)

COCHRANE-ORCUTT ITERATIVE TECHNIQUE

FINAL VALUE OF RHO=   -0.3197915
STANDARD ERROR OF RHO =   0.1934052

RIGHT-HAND VARIABLE	ESTIMATED COEFFICIENT	STANDARD ERROR	T-STATISTIC
CONST.	0.320572E-02	0.213298E-01	0.150293
DPROFS (3)	-0.267237E-01	0.177681	-0.150402
DPROFS (2)	0.177079	0.160938	1.10029
DPROFS (1)	-0.297120	0.164133	-1.81023
DPROFS	0.462750	0.160571	2.88191
DPROFS (-1)	-0.129523	0.161742	-0.800798
DPROFS (-2)	-0.167229	0.168283	-0.993732
DPROFS (-3)	-0.424410E-01	0.156021	-0.272022
DPROFS (-4)	-0.242211	0.155441	-1.55822

R-SQUARED = 0.637844   NOBS=   24
R-BAR-SQUARED (ADJ FOR DF)= 0.444694
DURBIN-WATSON (0 GAPS) = 1.937264

F - STATISTIC = 1.5

The F statistic tests the null hypothesis that the future coefficients of DPROFS are jointly equal to zero. The variable DPROFS measures the growth rate in net income/sales. If RS is defined as net income divided by sales, then DPROFS = (RS(t)-RS(t-1))/RS(t).

EQUATION 20

PILLSBURY MILLS INC.

DEPENDENT VARIABLE IS   (A(t)-A(t-1))/A(t)

THE CURRENTLY ACTIVE OBSERVATION SET IS
(1956- 1980)

COCHRANE-ORCUTT ITERATIVE TECHNIQUE

FINAL VALUE OF RHO=   -0.3197915
STANDARD ERROR OF RHO =   0.1934052

RIGHT-HAND VARIABLE	ESTIMATED COEFFICIENT	STANDARD ERROR	T-STATISTIC
CONST.	0.320572E-02	0.213298E-01	0.150293
DPROFS (3)	-0.267237E-01	0.177681	-0.150402
DPROFS (2)	0.177079	0.160938	1.10029
DPROFS (1)	-0.297120	0.164133	-1.81023
DPROFS	0.462750	0.160571	2.88191
DPROFS (-1)	-0.129523	0.161742	-0.800798
DPROFS (-2)	-0.167229	0.168283	-0.993732
DPROFS (-3)	-0.424410E-01	0.156021	-0.272022
DPROFS (-4)	-0.242211	0.155441	-1.55822

R-SQUARED = 0.637844   NOBS=   24
R-BAR-SQUARED (ADJ FOR DF)= 0.444694
DURBIN-WATSON (0 GAPS) = 1.937264

F - STATISTIC = 1.50

The F statistic tests the null hypothesis that the future coefficients of DPROFS are jointly equal to zero. The variable DPROFS measures the growth rate in net income/sales. If RS is defined as net income divided by sales, then DPROFS = (RS(t)-RS(t-1))/RS(t).

EQUATION 21

PROCTER AND GAMBLE

DEPENDENT VARIABLE IS   (A(t)-A(t-1))/A(t)

THE CURRENTLY ACTIVE OBSERVATION SET IS
(1956- 1980)

COCHRANE-ORCUTT ITERATIVE TECHNIQUE

FINAL VALUE OF RHO=   -0.3094184
STANDARD ERROR OF RHO =   0.1941070

RIGHT-HAND VARIABLE	ESTIMATED COEFFICIENT	STANDARD ERROR	T-STATISTIC
CONST.	-0.194101E-02	0.117560E-01	-0.165108
DPROFS (3)	-0.350804	0.274427	-1.27831
DPROFS (2)	-0.136910	0.345495	-0.396271
DPROFS (1)	-0.615316	0.409025	-1.50435
DPROFS	0.426297	0.401422	1.06197
DPROFS (-1)	-1.09871	0.376661	-2.91698
DPROFS (-2)	0.570871	0.310424	1.83900
DPROFS (-3)	-0.100750	0.249779	-0.403359

R-SQUARED =   0.557472   NOBS=   24
R-BAR-SQUARED (ADJ FOR DF)= 0.363866
DURBIN-WATSON (0 GAPS) = 1.999192

F - STATISTIC = 3.26

The F statistic tests the null hypothesis that the future
coefficients of DPROFS are jointly equal to zero. The variable
DPROFS measures the growth rate in net income/sales.   If RS is
defined   as   net   income divided by sales, then DPROFS =
(RS(t)-RS(t-1))/RS(t).

EQUATION 22

QUAKER OATS COMPANY

DEPENDENT VARIABLE IS   (A(t)-(At-1))/A(t)

THE CURRENTLY ACTIVE OBSERVATION SET IS
(1956- 1980)

COCHRANE-ORCUTT ITERATIVE TECHNIQUE

FINAL VALUE OF RHO=   -0.3816417
STANDARD ERROR OF RHO =   0.1886741

RIGHT-HAND VARIABLE	ESTIMATED COEFFICIENT	STANDARD ERROR	T-STATISTIC
CONST.	0.257737E-02	0.242466E-01	0.106298
DPROFS (3)	-0.392578	0.242315	-1.62011
DPROFS (2)	0.342422	0.258713	1.32356
DPROFS (1)	-0.787358	0.293277	-2.68469
DPROFS	0.243792	0.289207	0.842969
DPROFS (-1)	0.182056	0.281704	0.646266
DPROFS (-2)	-0.288248	0.255021	-1.13029
DPROFS (-3)	0.432272E-01	0.228245	0.189389

R-SQUARED =   0.561717   NOBS=   24
R-BAR-SQUARED (ADJ FOR DF)= 0.369969
DURBIN-WATSON (0 GAPS) = 1.918087

F STATISTIC = 2.32

The F statistic tests the null hypothesis that the future
coefficients of DPROFS are jointly equal to zero. The variable
DPROFS measures the growth rate in net income/sales.   If RS is
defined   as   net   income divided by sales, then DPROFS =
(RS(t)-RS(t-1))/RS(t).

EQUATION 23

RADIO CORPORATION OF AMERICA

DEPENDENT VARIABLE IS   (A(t)-A(t-1))/A(t)

THE CURRENTLY ACTIVE OBSERVATION SET IS
(1956- 1980)

ORDINARY LEAST SQUARES

RIGHT-HAND VARIABLE	ESTIMATED COEFFICIENT	STANDARD ERROR	T-STATISTIC
CONST.	-0.851339E-02	0.359066E-01	-0.237098
DPROFS (3)	-0.803811E-03	0.462414E-01	-0.173829E-01
DPROFS (2)	0.312804E-01	0.542807E-01	0.576271
DPROFS (1)	0.342660E-01	0.565977E-01	0.605431
DPROFS	-0.831497E-01	0.123415	-0.673739
DPROFS (-1)	0.455183	0.136863	3.32583
DPROFS (-2)	-0.188514	0.144458	-1.30497
DPROFS (-3)	0.727138E-01	0.150881	0.481929

R-SQUARED =   0.418110   NOBS=   25
R-BAR-SQUARED (ADJ FOR DF)= 0.178509
DURBIN-WATSON (0 GAPS) = 2.154328

F - STATISTIC = .22

The F statistic tests the null hypothesis that the future coefficients of DPROFS are jointly equal to zero. The variable DPROFS measures the growth rate in net income/sales. If RS is defined as net income divided by sales, then DPROFS = (RS(t)-RS(t-1))/RS(t).

EQUATION 24

REYNOLDS TOBACCO COMPANY

DEPENDENT VARIABLE IS   (A(t)-A(t-1))/A(t)

THE CURRENTLY ACTIVE OBSERVATION SET IS
(1956- 1980)

COCHRANE-ORCUTT ITERATIVE TECHNIQUE

FINAL VALUE OF RHO=   -0.2176040
STANDARD ERROR OF RHO =   0.1992327

RIGHT-HAND VARIABLE	ESTIMATED COEFFICIENT	STANDARD ERROR	T-STATISTIC
CONST.	-0.743847E-02	0.451204E-01	-0.164858
DPROFS (3)	1.00101	0.839831	1.19192
DPROFS (2)	0.313396	0.851528	0.368040
DPROFS (1)	-1.21768	0.986781	-1.23399
DPROFS	-0.931909	1.03160	-0.903363
DPROFS (-1)	0.149944	0.985339	0.152175
DPROFS (-2)	-0.744006	0.883298	-0.842305
DPROFS (-3)	0.395617	0.651047	0.607663

R-SQUARED =   0.300369   NOBS=   24
R-BAR-SQUARED (ADJ FOR DF)= -0.005719
DURBIN-WATSON (0 GAPS) = 2.152026

F - STATISTIC = .65

The F statistic tests the null hypothesis that the future coefficients of DPROFS are jointly equal to zero. The variable DPROFS measures the growth rate in net income/sales. If RS is defined as net income divided by sales, then DPROFS = (RS(t)-RS(t-1))/RS(t).

EQUATION 25

STERLING DRUG COMPANY

DEPENDENT VARIABLE IS   (A(t)-A(t-1))/A(t)

THE CURRENTLY ACTIVE OBSERVATION SET IS
(1956- 1980)

COCHRANE-ORCUTT ITERATIVE TECHNIQUE

FINAL VALUE OF RHO=   0.3218464
STANDARD ERROR OF RHO =   0.1932631

RIGHT-HAND VARIABLE	ESTIMATED COEFFICIENT	STANDARD ERROR	T-STATISTIC
CONST.	-0.355041E-01	0.405567E-01	-0.875419
DPROFS (3)	-1.19441	0.675827	-1.76733
DPROFS (2)	-1.10769	0.672113	-1.64807
DPROFS (1)	-0.314196E-01	0.656230	-0.478789E-01
DPROFS	-0.440338	0.669362	-0.657848
DPROFS (-1)	0.530033	0.667028	0.794619
DPROFS (-2)	-0.399572	0.580984	-0.687751
DPROFS (-3)	-0.639334E-01	0.526338	-0.121468
DPROFS (-4)	-0.449182	0.510095	-0.880585

R-SQUARED = 0.437162 NOBS=   24
R-BAR-SQUARED (ADJ FOR DF)= 0.136982
DURBIN-WATSON (0 GAPS) = 1.850756

F - STATISTIC = 1.53

The F statistic tests the null hypothesis that the future coefficients of DPROFS are jointly equal to zero. The variable DPROFS measures the growth rate in net income/sales. If RS is defined as net income divided by sales, then DPROFS = (RS(t)-RS(t-1))/RS(t).

EQUATION 26

WARNER-LAMBERT PHARMACEUTICAL

DEPENDENT VARIABLE IS   (A(t)-A(t-1))/A(t)

THE CURRENTLY ACTIVE OBSERVATION SET IS
(1956- 1980)

ORDINARY LEAST SQUARES

RIGHT-HAND VARIABLE	ESTIMATED COEFFICIENT	STANDARD ERROR	T-STATISTIC
CONST.	-0.309172E-01	0.394713E-01	-0.783284
DPROFS (3)	-0.349280E-02	0.101247E-01	-0.344977
DPROFS (2)	0.525449E-02	0.152764E-01	0.343962
DPROFS (1)	-0.800715E-02	0.171049E-01	-0.468120
DPROFS	-0.620333E-01	0.195753	-0.316896
DPROFS (-1)	0.146412	0.242807	0.602996
DPROFS (-2)	0.169723	0.284232	0.597129
DPROFS (-3)	-0.114989	0.258455	-0.444909
DPROFS (-4)	-0.338893	0.226746	-1.49459
DPROFS (-5)	0.118550	0.114013	1.03979

R-SQUARED = 0.226401 NOBS=   25
R-BAR-SQUARED (ADJ FOR DF)= -0.237759
DURBIN-WATSON (0 GAPS) = 1.770050

F - STATISTIC = .18

The F statistic tests the null hypothesis that the future coefficients of DPROFS are jointly equal to zero. The variable DPROFS measures the growth rate in net income/sales. If RS is defined as net income divided by sales, then DPROFS = (RS(t)-RS(t-1))/RS(t).

EQUATION 27

WILLIAM WRIGLEY JR. COMPANY

DEPENDENT VARIABLE IS   (A(t)-A(t-1))/A(t)

THE CURRENTLY ACTIVE OBSERVATION SET IS
(1956- 1980)

COCHRANE-ORCUTT ITERATIVE TECHNIQUE

FINAL VALUE OF RHO=   -0.3741040
STANDARD ERROR OF RHO =   0.1893020

RIGHT-HAND VARIABLE	ESTIMATED COEFFICIENT	STANDARD ERROR	T-STATISTIC
CONST.	0.335003E-01	0.212700E-01	1.57500
DPROFS (3)	0.721997	0.297456	2.42724
DPROFS (2)	0.453831	0.298848	1.51860
DPROFS (1)	0.322554	0.322536	1.00006
DPROFS	0.876752	0.317236	2.76372
DPROFS (-1)	-0.570616	0.363498	-1.56979
DPROFS (-2)	-0.964995	0.367858	-2.62328
DPROFS (-3)	0.162433	0.358130	0.453558
DPROFS (-4)	-1.02635	0.354060	-2.89880
DPROFS (-5)	-0.534179	0.343956	-1.55305

R-SQUARED =   0.756549   NOBS=   24
R-BAR-SQUARED (ADJ FOR DF)= 0.600045
DURBIN-WATSON (0 GAPS) = 2.157039

F - STATISTIC = 2.58

The F statistic tests the null hypothesis that the future coefficients of DPROFS are jointly equal to zero. The variable DPROFS measures the growth rate in net income/sales. If RS is defined as net income divided by sales, then DPROFS = (RS(t)-RS(t-1))/RS(t).

References

Albion, Mark S. and Farris, Paul W. 1979. "Appraising Research on Advertising's Economic Impacts." Marketing Science Institute (Cambridge, Mass.), report no. 79-115 (December).

———. 1981. *The Advertising Controversy* (Boston: Auburn House).

Ashley, R.; Granger, C.W.J.; and Schmalensee, R. 1980. "Advertising and Aggregate Consumption: An Analysis of Causality." *Econometrica* 48 (July): 1149–67.

Ayanian, Robert. 1975. "Advertising and Rate of Return." *Journal of Law and Economics* 18 (October): 479–506.

———. 1983. "The Advertising Capital Controversy." *Journal of Business* 56 (April): 349–64.

Bain, Joe S. 1956. *Barriers to New Competition* (Cambridge, Mass.: Harvard University Press).

Baldani, J. and Masson, R.T. 1984. "Economies of Scale, Strategic Advertising and Fully Credible Entry Deterrence." *Review of Industrial Organization* 1 (Fall): 190–205.

Baumol, William J.; Panzar, John C.; and Willig, Robert D. 1982. *Contestable Markets and the Theory of Industry Structure* (New York: Harcourt Brace Jovanovich).

Baye, Michael R. 1981. "Optimal Adjustments to Changes in the Price of Advertising." *Journal of Industrial Economics* 30 (September): 95–103.

———. 1983. "Optimal Adjustments to Restrictions on Advertising: Some Further Comments." *Journal of Industrial Economics* 32 (December): 249–51.

Bishop, John A. and Yoo, Jang H. 1985. "Health Scare, Excise Taxes and Advertising Ban in the Cigarette Demand and Supply." *Southern Economic Journal* 52 (October): 402–11.

Bloch, Harry. 1974. "Advertising and Profitability: A Reappraisal." *Journal of Political Economy* 82 (March): 267–86.

———. 1980. "The Effect of Advertising on Competition: Comments on a Survey." *Journal of Economic Literature* 18 (September): 1063–66.

Brown, Randall S. 1978. "Estimating Advantages to Large Scale Advertising." *Review of Economics and Statistics* 60 (August): 428–37.

Butters, Gerard R. 1977. "Equilibrium Distributions of Sales and Advertising Prices." *Review of Economic Studies* 44 (October): 465–91.

Caves, Richard E. and Williamson, Peter J. 1985. "What is Product Differentiation, Really?" *Journal of Industrial Economics* 34 (December): 113–32.

Clarke, Darral G. 1976. "Econometric Measurement of the Duration of Advertising Effect on Sales." *Journal of Marketing Research* 13 (November): 345–57.

Clarke, R. and Else, P.K. 1983. "Optimal Adjustments to Restrictions on Advertising: A Comment." *Journal of Industrial Economics* 32 (December): 243–48.

Comanor, William S. and Wilson, Thomas A. 1974. *Advertising and Market Power* (Cambridge, Mass.: Harvard University Press).

———. 1979. "The Effect of Advertising on Competition: A Survey." *Journal of Economic Literature* 17 (June): 453–76.

———. 1980. "On the Economics of Advertising: A Reply to Bloch and Simon." *Journal of Economic Literature* 18 (September): 1075–78.

Cubbin, John. 1981. "Advertising and the Theory of Entry Barriers." *Economica* 48 (August): 289–99.

Demsetz, Harold. 1973. "Industry Structure, Market Rivalry, and Public Policy." *Journal of Law and Economics* 16 (April): 1–9.

———. 1979. "Accounting for Advertising as a Barrier to Entry." *Journal of Business* July: 345–60.

———. 1982. "Barriers to Entry." *American Economic Review* 72 (March): 47–57.

Dixit, Avinash K. 1980. "The Role of Investment in Entry Deterrence." *Economic Journal* 90 (March): 95–106.

———. 1982. "Recent Developments in Oligopoly Theory." *American Economic Review* 72 (May): 12–17.

Dixit, Avinash K. and Norman, Victor D. 1978. "Advertising and Welfare." *Bell Journal of Economics* 9 (Spring): 1–17.

———. 1979. "Advertising and Welfare: Reply." *Bell Journal of Economics* 10 (Autumn): 728–29.

———. 1980. "Advertising and Welfare: Another Reply." *Bell Journal of Economics* 11 (Autumn): 753–54.

Dorfman, Robert and Steiner, Peter O. 1954. "Optimal Advertising and Optimal Quality." *American Economic Review* 44 (December): 826–36.

Doron, Gideon. 1979. *The Smoking Paradox* (Cambridge, Mass.: Abt Books).

Ehrlich, I. and Fisher, L. 1982. "The Derived Demand for Advertising: A Theoretical and Empirical Investigation." *American Economic Review* 72 (June): 366–88.

Farris, Paul W. 1978. "Advertising in Consumer Goods Businesses: An Empirical Analysis." *Marketing Science Institute* (Cambridge, Mass.), report no. 78-118 (December).

——— and Albion, Mark S. 1980. "Determinants of Variations in the Advertising-to-Sales Ratio: A Comparison of Industry and Firm Studies." Marketing Science Institute (Cambridge, Mass.), report no. 80-107 (October).

——— and Buzzell, Robert D. 1976. "Relationships Between Changes in Industrial Advertising and Promotion Expenditures and Changes in Market Share." Marketing Science Institute (Cambridge, Mass.), report no. 76-119 (December).

——— and Reibstein, David J. 1978. "Using a Nonlinear Response Function in Estimating Advertising's Carry-Over Effects." Marketing Science Institute (Cambridge, Mass.), report no. 78-107 (August).

Ferguson, James M. 1974. *Advertising and Competition: Theory, Measurement, Fact* (Cambridge, Mass.: Ballinger Publishing).

Fisher, Franklin M. 1979. "Diagnosing Monopoly." *Quarterly Review of Economics and Business* 19 (Summer): 7–33.

————. 1984. "The Misuse of Accounting Rates of Return: Reply." *American Economic Review* 74 (June): 509–17.

————. 1986. "One the Misuse of the Profit–Sales Ratio to Infer Monopoly Power." M.I.T. working paper E52-359 (April).

Fisher, Franklin M. and McGowan, John J. 1979. "Advertising and Welfare: Comment." *Bell Journal of Economics* 10 (Autumn): 726–27.

————. 1983. "On the Misuse of Accounting Rates of Return to Infer Monopoly Profits." *American Economic Review* 73 (March): 82–97.

Fudenberg, Drew and Tirole, Jean. 1984. "The Fat-Cat Effect, the Puppy-Dog Ploy, and the Lean and Hungry Look." *American Economic Review* 74 (May): 361–66.

Geweke, John. 1978. "Testing the Exogeneity Specification in the Complete Dynamic Simultaneous Equation Model." *Journal of Econometrics* 7 (April): 163–85.

————; Meese, Richard; and Dent, Warren. 1983. "Comparing Alternative Tests of Causality in Temporal Systems: Analytic Results and Experimental Evidence." *Journal of Econometrics* 21 (February): 161–94.

Granger, C.W.J. 1969. "Investigating Causal Relations by Econometric Models and Cross-Spectral Methods." *Econometrica* 37 (July): 424–38.

Grossman, Gene M. and Shapiro, Carl. 1984. "Informative Advertising with Differentiated Products." *Review of Economic Studies* 51 (January): 63–81.

Hamilton, J.L. 1972. "The Demand for Cigarettes: Advertising, the Health Scare and the Cigarette Advertising Ban." *Review of Economics and Statistics* 54 (November): 401–11.

Harvey, A.C. 1981. *The Econometric Analysis of Time Series* (New York: Halsted Press).

Henderson, James M. and Quandt, Richard E. 1971. *Microeconomic Theory: A Mathematical Approach* (New York: McGraw-Hill).

Henning, John A. and Mann, H. Michael. 1976. "Advertising and Concentration: A Tentative Determination of Cause and Effect." In *Essays of Industrial Organization in Honor of Joe S. Bain,* edited by R.T. Masson and P.D. Qualls (Cambridge, Mass.: Ballinger Publishing): 143–54.

Horowitz, Ira. 1970. "A Note on Advertising and Uncertainty." *Journal of Industrial Economics* 19 (April): 151–60.

Hsiao, Cheng. 1981. "Autoregressive Modelling and Money–Income Causality Detection." *Journal of Monetary Economics* 7 (January): 85–106.

Johnson, Paul R. 1984. *The Economics of the Tobacco Industry* (New York: Praeger Publishers).

Judge, George G.; Griffiths, William E.; Hill, R. Carter; and Lee, Tsoung-Chao. 1980. *The Theory and Practice of Econometrics* (New York: John Wiley and Sons).

Kaldor, Nicholas. 1950. "The Economic Aspects of Advertising." *Review of Economic Studies* 18: 1–27.

Kihlstrom, Richard E. and Riordan, Michael H. 1984. "Advertising as a Signal." *Journal of Political Economy* 92 (June): 427–50.

Kmenta, Jan. 1986. *Elements of Econometrics* (New York: MacMillan Publishing Company).

Kotowitz, Yehuda and Mathewson, Frank. 1979. "Advertising, Consumer Information and Product Quality." *Bell Journal of Economics* 10 (Autumn): 566–88.

———. 1980. "Informative Advertising and Welfare." *American Economic Review.* 69 (June): 284–94.

Lambin, Jean Jacques. 1976. *Advertising, Competition and Market Conduct in Oligopoly Over Time* (Amsterdam: North-Holland Publishing).

Lewit, Eugene M.; Coate, Douglas; and Grossman, Michael. 1981. "The Effects of Government Regulation on Teenage Smoking." *Journal of Law and Economics* 24 (December): 545–70.

Long, William F. and Ravenscraft, David J. 1984. "The Misuse of Accounting Rates of Return: Comment." *American Economic Review* 74 (June): 494–500.

Martin, Stephen. 1984. "The Misuse of Accounting Rates of Return: Comment." *American Economic Review* 74 (June): 501–6.

———. 1985. "The Measurement of Profitability and the Diagnosis of Market Power: I." Michigan state working paper (April).

McLeod, Paul B. 1986. "Advertising Bans, Tobacco and Cigarette Consumption." *Economics Letters* 20: 391–96.

Nagle, Thomas T. 1981. "Do Advertising-Profitability Studies Really Show That Advertising Creates a Barrier to Entry?" *Journal of Law and Economics* 24 (October): 333–49.

Needham, Douglas. 1976. "Entry Barriers and Non-Price Aspects of Firms' Behavior." *Journal of Industrial Economics* 25 (September): 29–43.

Nelson, Philip. 1970. "Information and Consumer Behavior." *Journal of Political Economy* 78 (April): 311–29.

———. 1974. "Advertising as Information." *Journal of Political Economy* 82 (July): 729–54.

———. 1978. "Advertising as Information Once More." In *Issues in Advertising,* edited by David G. Tuerck. American Enterprise Institute, 133–61.

Netters, Jeffry M. 1982. "Excessive Advertising: An Empirical Analysis. *Journal of Industrial Economics* 30 (June): 361–73.

Nichols, Len M. 1985. "Advertising and Economic Welfare." *American Economic Review* 75 (March): 213–18.

Ornstein, Stanley I. 1975. "Empirical Uses of the Price–Cost Margin." *Journal of Industrial Economics* 24 (December): 105–17.

———. 1976. "The Advertising-Concentration Controversy." *Southern Economic Journal* 42 (July): 892–902.

———. 1977. *Industrial Concentration and Advertising Intensity.* (American Enterprise Institute).

Pagoulatos, Emilio and Sorensen, Robert. 1981. "A Simultaneous Equation Analysis of Advertising, Concentration and Profitability." *Southern Economic Journal* 47 (January): 728–41.

Peles, Yoram. 1971. "Rates of Amortization of Advertising Expenditures." *Journal of Political Economy* 79 (September): 1032–58.

Porter, Michael E. 1978. "Optimal Advertising: An Intra-Industry Approach." In *Issues in Advertising,* edited by David G. Tuerck. American Enterprise Institute.

Rogerson, William P. 1984. "A Note on the Incentive for a Monopolist to Increase Fixed Costs as a Barrier to Entry." *Quarterly Journal of Economics* 99 (May): 399–402.

Salop, Steven C. 1979. "Strategic Entry Deterrence." *American Economic Review* 69 (May): 335–38.

—— and Scheffman, David T. 1983. "Raising Rivals' Costs." *American Economic Review* 73 (May): 267–72.

Scherer, F.M. 1980. *Industrial Market Structure and Economic Performance* (Chicago: Rand McNally College Publishing Company).

Schmalensee, Richard. 1972. *The Economics of Advertising* (Amsterdam: North-Holland Publishing).

——. 1974. "Brand Loyalty and Barriers to Entry." *Southern Economic Journal* 40 (April): 579–88.

——. 1976. "Advertising and Profitability." *Journal of Industrial Economics* 25 (September): 45–54.

——. 1978. "A Model of Advertising and Product Quality." *Journal of Political Economy* 86 (June): 485–503.

——. 1983. "Advertising and Entry Deterrence: An Exploratory Model." *Journal of Political Economy* 91 (August): 636–53.

——, Silk, Alvin J., and Bojanek, Robert. 1983. "The Impact of Scale and Media Mix on Advertising Agency Costs." *Journal of Business* 56 (June): 453–75.

Schneider, Lynne; Klein, Benjamin; and Murphy, Kevin M. 1981. "Governmental Regulation of Cigarette Health Information." *Journal of Law and Economics* 24 (December): 575–612.

Schramm, Richard and Sherman, Roger. 1976. "Advertising to Manage Profit Risk." *Journal of Industrial Economics* 25 (June): 295–311.

Shapiro, Carl. 1980. "Advertising and Welfare: Comment." *Bell Journal of Economics* 11 (Autumn): 749–52.

Sherman, Roger and Tollison, Robert. 1971. "Advertising and Profitability." *Review of Economics and Statistics* 53 (November): 397–407.

——. 1972. "Technology, Profit Risk, and Assessments of Market Performance." *Quarterly Journal of Economics* 86 (August): 448–62.

Simon, Julian L. 1965. "Are There Economies of Scale in Advertising?" *Journal of Advertising Research* 5 (June): 15–20.

——. 1970. *Issues in the Economics of Advertising.* (Urbana: University of Illinois Press).

——. 1980. "On Firm Size and Advertising Efficiency: A Comment." *Journal of Economic Literature* 18 (September): 1066–75.

Simon, Julian L. and Arndt, Johan. 1980. "The Shape of the Advertising Response Function and Economies of Scale: A Review of the Empirical Evidence." *Journal of Advertising Research* 20 (August): 11–28.

——. 1983. "Advertising and Economies of Scale: Critical Comments on the Evidence." *Journal of Industrial Economics* 32 (December): 229–42.

Sims, Christopher A. 1972. "Money, Income, and Causality." *American Economic Review* 62 (September): 540–52.

——. 1977. "Exogeneity and Causal Ordering in Macroeconomic Models." In *New Methods of Business Cycle Research: Proceedings from a Conference,* edited by C.A. Sims. Federal Reserve Bank of Minneapolis.

Skoog, Gary R. 1976. "Causality Characterizations: Bivariate, Trivariate, and Multivariate Propositions." Federal Reserve Bank of Minneapolis, staff report no. 14 (November).

Spence, Michael A. 1977. "Entry, Capacity, Investment and Oligopolistic Pricing." *Bell Journal of Economics* 8 (Autumn): 534–44.

———. 1980. "Notes on Advertising, Economies of Scale, and Entry Barriers." *Quarterly Journal of Economics* 95 (November): 493–507.

Stigler, George J. 1983. *The Organization of Industry* (Chicago: University of Chicago Press).

——— and Becker, Gary S. 1977. "De Gustibus Non Est Disputandum." *American Economic Review* 67 (March): 76–90.

Strickland, Allyn P. and Weiss, Leonard W. 1976. "Advertising, Concentration and Price Cost Margins." *Journal of Political Economy* 84 (October): 1109–21.

Sullivan, Daniel. 1985. "Testing Hypotheses about Firm Behavior in the Cigarette Industry." *Journal of Political Economy* 93 (June): 586–98.

Sumner, Daniel A. 1981. "Measurement of Monopoly Behavior: An Application to the Cigarette Industry." *Journal of Political Economy* 89 (October): 1010–19.

Telser, Lester G. 1969. "Comment." *American Economic Review* 59 (May): 121–23.

———. 1978. "Towards a Theory of the Economics of Advertising." In *Issues in Advertising,* edited by David G. Tuerck. American Enterprise Institute.

van Breda, Michael F. 1984. "The Misuse of Accounting Rates of Return: Comment." *American Economic Review* 74 (June): 507–8.

Varian, Hal R. 1978. *Microeconomic Analysis* (New York: W.W. Norton and Co.).

Vernon, John; Rives, N.W.; and Naylor, T.H. 1969. "An Econometric Model of the Tobacco Industry." *Review of Economics and Statistics* (May): 149–58.

von Weizsacker, C.C. 1980. "A Welfare Analysis of Barriers to Entry." *Bell Journal of Economics* 11 (Fall): 399–420.

Weiss, Leonard W. 1974. "The Concentration–Profits Relationship and Antitrust." In *Industrial Concentration: the New Learning,* edited by Harvey J. Goldschmid et al, 184–233. (Boston: Little, Brown and Company).

Wu, De-Min. 1983. "Tests of Causality, Predeterminedness and Exogeneity." *International Economic Review* 24 (October): 547–57.

Zellner, Arnold. 1979. "Causality and Econometrics." *Carnegie–Rochester Conference Series on Public Policy* 10.

Index

About the Author

Robert E. McAuliffe is an assistant professor of economics at Babson College in Wellesley, Massachusetts. He has published articles on monetary theory in the *Eastern Economic Journal* and the *American Economist*. He received his B.A. from Colby College and his Ph.D. from the University of Virginia.